MW01487845

THE Z FACTOR

THE Z FACTOR

HOW TO LEAD GEN Z TO WORKPLACE SUCCESS

ROHIN SHAHI

NEW DEGREE PRESS

COPYRIGHT © 2019 ROHIN SHAHI

All rights reserved.

THE Z FACTOR

How to Lead Gen Z to Workplace Success

ISBN   978-1-64137-355-5   *Paperback*

          978-1-64137-690-7   *Ebook*

CONTENTS

INTRODUCTION

Every time a new generation enters the workplace, older generations let out a collective groan. Writers spit out dozens of books and articles about how the workplace is crumbling, volcanoes erupt, and angels cry. But with enough time, these lamentations prove to be far from the truth.

Remember when millennials entered the workforce, and everyone was confused? Simply put, there was a disconnect: millennials said they wanted X, companies offered Y, and what actually happened was Z. As a result, there was a huge productivity drain, lack of engagement, and high employee turnover that largely contributed to them being labeled the "Job-Hopping Generation." However, companies that were able to adapt more quickly to the needs of this new generation had a competitive leg up by attracting talented millennials and fostering a productive working environment for them.

It's a cyclical effect that happens when each generation enters the workplace. "Gen Xers have a poor work ethic." "Millennials are entitled." "Gen Zers are glued to their phones." The truth is that each generation is unique in their perspectives and experiences, and this causes a lack of understanding by other generations. Over time, painstakingly slowly, more senior workers begin to understand the needs and wants of that generation. But by the time that happens, a new generation has entered the workplace, and the cycle of unpreparedness continues.

But what if that wasn't the case? What if we took the time to proactively prepare and crafted a workplace that allows the newest generation to flourish? It's an idea that could save us millions of dollars of research and countless hours of trial-and-error as soon as we begin to work.

Gen Z is now entering the job market, and we're the largest generation ever, making up 32 percent of the world's population. We're poised to make an unprecedented impact on the world, but only with the right guidance.

That's the purpose of this book. Whether you're a manager, a recruiter, a startup founder, or even a Gen Zer curious about how we're going to impact the workplace, this book is aimed toward you.

It's aimed to shake off the preconception that my generation is made up of mindless drones held captive by our devices. I want to show what makes us tick. What motivates us? What outlook do we have on life? By learning this, you can cultivate a work environment that we want to work at, attracting and retaining loyal and eager new talent.

The book is divvied up so that each chapter is about a unique aspect of our generation. For instance, there's a chapter about our entrepreneurial spirit, and another about our desire for stability. But beyond simply stating things about us, the book details steps that companies, HR professionals, and managers can take to ease Gen Z's transition into the workplace, resulting in more engaged and happier employees.

One thing you'll probably notice is how intertwined each of the traits and themes are. For example, the second chapter begins by talking about entrepreneurship, but it references Gen Zers' desire for flexibility, our practicality, and the technology we've grown up around. This highlights that all of these characteristics aren't disparate elements, but rather come together to make up a truly unique map of who we are as a generation.

It's important to note that generational research isn't perfect. Most studies are American surveys where Gen Z participants are from middle- or upper-class families. Conclusions drawn in this book don't apply to each and every person, but serve as rough guidelines for who we are. For instance, Gen Z tends to be more innovative and entrepreneurial than other generations, but that doesn't mean every Gen Zer wants to be a startup owner. Everything I say in this book is meant to highlight trends of this generation, but we're all unique individuals with our own dispositions and outlooks on life. Rather than putting an entire generation into a sealed-off box, I want to highlight trends important for leading this next generation of workers.

Ultimately, the goal is to humanize Gen Z. Too many articles, books, and speakers on generational research use broad generalizations to make bold assertions about who we are. This book, drawing upon new research and interviews with experts, isn't an end-all-be-all, but rather a tool to better understand people and be a little smarter about how we incorporate this next generation into the workplace.

Each chapter has key takeaways listed at the end. There's a lot of information packed into this book, and so this will help in understanding the most important points of each chapter. Plus, it'll help if you decide to revisit the book and just skim through the major pointers.

This is my first book, and I'm really excited to have the opportunity to share my perspective, new research, and the insight of experts with you. Thank you!

WHAT MAKES GENERATIONS DIFFERENT?

———

Before really digging into what makes Gen Z tick, I think our first step is to analyze the generations currently in the workforce. After all, we were raised and guided by older generations, and many of their values have shaped us.

The age ranges for generations are debated, and so I'll be using parameters set by the Pew Research Center, a fact tank based in Washington, DC, and a leader in generational studies.[1] Much of the generational research is also from Pew (I

———

1   "Generations And Age," 2019, *Pew Research Center.*

want to avoid bombarding this chapter with citations from the same place). We'll start with the oldest generation currently in the workforce. They're called the silent generation, but its members are referred to as traditionalists.

They were born between 1928 and 1945. This is largely why they're called the silent generation: they were too young to fight in World War II, but too old to be part of the boomer generation. For the large part, having grown up in times of war and crisis, they learned to be tight-lipped and cautious. Traditionalists, at least compared to younger generations, rarely have revolutionary beliefs, preferring to stick with existing systems. All-in-all, they are, well, traditional, seeking financial well-being and security. This mentality shaped their work ethic throughout their careers.

Traditionalist children were brought up in a post-Depression world, and so were taught to work hard and keep their heads down. They're a comparatively small generation, since parents were worried about financial security and had less children. Despite the poor economic conditions of their childhood, the post-war job market was booming when they entered the workforce, and when adjusting for inflation, they were paid very well. They are very loyal employees, as many worked at the same company for much of their lives. They respect authority, and now that they tend to hold senior-level positions, expect the same in return.

As recently as a few years ago, most people retired in their sixties, but today's a new day. With people living longer, it's become necessary for many to keep on working. Plus, many traditionalists simply like working. As a result, there are still many working today, though all (or close to all) will retire within a few years.

In today's hyperconnected world, traditionalists may have a lot of trouble with technology. They oftentimes don't have the same innate understanding of tech as younger generations do and can feel almost "left behind" if not kept in the loop. For instance, while many traditionalists know how to use email, it can be more effective to talk in-person or over the phone.

They make up a small fraction of the workforce today—approximately 2 percent as of this writing. This leads us to the second-oldest generation in the workforce today: baby boomers.

The boomers were born between 1946 and 1964. They grew up post-World War II in a time of huge economic expansion, and as the name suggests, there's a lot of them. In America, the GI Bill allowed many veterans to settle down and raise families. The average age of marriages dropped, and the population exploded. This had an adverse effect of causing a scarcity of resources; competition for colleges and jobs was fierce at first.[2]

The '60s and '70s marked a distinct change between boomers and older generations. Between cultural shifts and social movements such as civil rights marches, it quickly became clear that they were far more rebellious and idealistic than previous generations.[3]

With this optimism came a more curious and change-seeking mindset, valuing open communication and asking questions to better the workplace. This is when traditional views on work began to fall apart. Instead of simply being a means for making money, boomers began to view work as a method of self-expression. It's a big reason why, when meeting someone for the first time, we typically ask, "What do you do for a living?" Work has become tied with our identities, and boomers felt empowered by this.

As of now, boomers hold the majority of senior level and executive positions. They act as mentors for younger generations and have a similar work ethic as traditionalists. Many boomers are quite technologically-savvy, but (especially when compared to younger generations) are still behind. In

---

2   "Baby Boom Generation," 2019.
3   Ibid.

short, boomers have a range of familiarity with tech; some are much better than others. Emails and PowerPoint presentations are familiar tools, but newer tech can have a big learning curve. Given recent economic dips such as the dotcom bubble bursting and the Great Recession, they are, for the large part, still working and make up roughly a third of the workforce. This fraction continues to drop, especially due to a relatively strong global economy in recent years.[4]

Generation X is a small generation that is oftentimes overlooked in generational research by the huge cohorts of boomers preceding them and millennials following. They mark a birth decline following the baby boom, but are soon to take up the mantle of senior management from retiring boomers. They were born between 1965 and 1980 and, for the most part, are defined by their flexibility, both in how they approach work and what they expect to get out of work. The concept of a work-life balance was really cemented by Gen X parents.

They get a bit of a bad reputation of being apathetic and cynical by nature. I talked to Aaron Paquette, Executive VP of the Television Group at Screen Engine/ASI and a career market researcher who specializes in media and entertainment. "A lot of the work that I've done over the years focused

---

4   Richard Fry, 2019, "Baby Boomers Are Staying In The Labor Force At Rates Not Seen In Generations For People Their Age," *Pew Research Center.*

on [coming up with] the most innovative research techniques to engage with [different generations]," said Aaron. Having worked extensively with different generations, he noticed that others among his generation, Gen X, did exhibit "classic Gen Xer" mentalities. They were "a little more cynical, a little more snarky . . . there was always some cynicism about the boss and the company."

It's a bit ironic that the "forgotten generation" is the most impactful generation for Generation Z. Why? Because they're our parents—nearly all Gen Zers are raised by Gen Xers. Upbringing is one of the biggest—if not *the* biggest—influencers that shape a generation's outlook. Gen X's more cynical and practical approach to life has definitely rubbed off on Gen Z, something we'll really dive into in later chapters.

That being said, it wouldn't be fair to simply label Gen X as cynical. As mentioned, they largely heralded the concept of a work-life balance, having noticed that their traditionalist (and older baby boomer) parents were burning out fast. Especially in America, where a traditional career path is oftentimes life-encompassing, it was necessary to bring attention to the negatives of being completely absorbed in careers while still striving for success.[5]

---

5   Sally Kane, 2019, "Learn The Common Characteristics Of Generation X Professionals," *The Common Characteristics Of Generation X Professionals.*

This leads us to oh-so-familiar millennials. They're quite possibly the least understood and most talked-about generation yet. Even now, decades after they entered the workplace, millennials have little support from older generations due to a fundamental lack of understanding of what millennials want from employers. Not only does this cause a barrier between generations in the workplace, but leads to negative stereotyping that can hinder millennials' professional growth.

Some of this stereotyping has gotten so bad that millennials themselves believe it. I've met multiple millennials who say, "Gosh, I hate my generation so much." They've been labeled as lazy, entitled, and narcissistic. To begin with, these stereotypes don't have much merit—millennials work as hard, if not harder, than previous generations did at their age, something fueled by the student debt epidemic and a desire to avoid continuing to drown in this debt.

And beyond this, there's simply a different work culture now. Take criticism of millennials' frequent job-hopping, for example. Millennials aren't switching jobs simply because they aren't satisfied with their current jobs or they want higher compensation elsewhere (though these are valid reasons, obviously), but also because the corporate environment is way different than decades ago. For a number of reasons, including an increasingly competitive job market and rapidly-changing job roles, no longer can an employee expect to join a company and stay there for years and years, steadily climbing the corporate ladder. A lot of the time, job-hopping is a survival mechanism in an increasingly competitive workplace.

"There is such a negative view in our society of this age group, that they are lazy or don't work hard, and yet there is no evidence of it whatsoever," said Jeffrey Jensen Arnett, PhD, who researches emerging adulthood at Clark University. "What is true is that they have high expectations of work, that they expect it to be more than just bringing home a paycheck. They are looking for identity-based work, something they enjoy that suits their abilities and interests."[6]

Millennials were born between 1981 and 1996 and are now well into adulthood.[7] They grew up during the dot-com boom as many new technologies and services were being created, and so are very digitally savvy. Having been raised by baby boomer parents with a "You can do anything you set your mind to" mentality, they grew up to be very idealistic during a time of economic expansion. Then the recession hit them like a dump truck, so that idealism was shredded apart.

---

6   Jaime Chamberlin, 2009, "Overgeneralizing The Generations," *American Psychological Association.*
7   "The Generations Defined," 2019, *Pew Research Center.*

At the time of writing this, I found common sentiments about each generation simply through Google searches. After typing "baby boomers are . . ." I let autocomplete fill in the rest.

For baby boomers, the most common searches were "baby boomers are selfish," "baby boomers are entitled," and "baby boomers are the problem." I thought that last one was a bit harsh, but it just goes to show that negativity and stereotyping doesn't just flow from older generations to younger ones; it's quite vicious the other way around, too, and causes generational divides to deepen further. (As a side note, some of these searches were pretty funny. "Millennials are killing cable." And golf. And mayo? And the doorbell industry.)

If these assumptions really manifest themselves within the workplace, there's poor decision-making all-around. "Oh, Jim's young. He'll probably enjoy working from home." Generational trends are just trends, not cookie-cutter guidelines. An overreliance on generational observations, especially wrong ones, can do more harm than good.

For the rest of the book, I'll be highlighting some of our values and principles, but not necessarily claiming, for instance, that every Gen Zer wants to be an entrepreneur, or that we all have a burning desire to out-muscle our peers and be crowned CEO of whatever company. Ultimately, this book is a tool, offering tips on making the workplace more inclusive and productive for us. I think we're a pretty cool generation (though I might be biased in saying so) and hope that you'll have a more accurate picture of who we are by the end of this book.

ENTREPRENEURSHIP AND SIDE HUSTLES

———

Picture an entrepreneur. Maybe you think of a college kid writing lines of code in his messy dorm room, pausing to chug from the nearest can of Red Bull. Maybe you imagine a well-dressed serial entrepreneur stepping out of a sports car to deliver a keynote speech. Some of the more cynical might think of the millions of unemployed people who write "Entrepreneur" on their LinkedIn (and dating) profiles.

Personally, I feel like nothing screams "entrepreneur" more than Elon Musk shooting a Tesla into space. But the point is that entrepreneurs come from all walks of life, and that's why no book or article has been able to (truthfully) say, "This is the archetypal entrepreneur, and here's exactly how you can become one."

However, after a lot of research, I've sketched up a model that highlights how entrepreneurs are made. I've broken it down below:

People with Entrepreneurial Spirit ⟶ Entrepreneurs

To summarize it, people who possess "entrepreneurial spirit" are more likely than others to become entrepreneurs. Jokes aside, at the very core, the only people who can become entrepreneurs are those who have the mindset necessary to actively seek out change rather than accept the status quo.

Gen Zers have this entrepreneurial spirit in spades, more than any generation in the past. A wide-scale attraction toward entrepreneurship began with millennials and is even stronger among Gen Zers today. According to a survey in 2014, 72 percent of high school students said they want to start a business someday.[8] Now, these same Gen Zers are in college and are just starting to enter the workforce.

Just to be clear, Gen Z is interested in both entrepreneurial ventures and small business ownership. The difference

---

8   Dan Schawbel, 2014, "The High School Careers Study," *millennialbranding.com.*

boils down to risk and the issues being solved. Entrepreneurs dream big and aim to solve pressing issues; their goals are lofty and risky but rewarding. Small business owners aim to solve a need, oftentimes in the community, and inherently take on less risk in doing so. Think high-growth startup versus a home appliances store. To keep things simpler, I'll be using the term entrepreneurship to denote both entrepreneurship and small business ownership for the rest of this book.

When I was young, around five or six, I remember sitting in front of the TV and watching an episode of SpongeBob SquarePants. It's a pretty famous and oft-referenced episode where SpongeBob and his friend Patrick Star become entrepreneurs by selling chocolate bars door-to-door. It was my first exposure to the term "entrepreneur," and that word became more and more relevant as I grew older.

In the second grade, we had an end of year "Extravaganza." Each student set up a booth in the cafeteria and sold wares to other students in exchange for fake money. Some offered products, like candy, and others sold services, like colored hair spraying. It was a very fun event, and students had the chance to experience a snippet of what it was like to be an entrepreneur. My mom and I painted ordinary rocks with pretty patterns and designs, and I sold them for exorbitant prices (see "Second Graders Have a Poor Understanding of

Money"). Through charging insane prices, I had better sales than any other student. It's my proudest achievement.

Entrepreneurship was a huge buzzword in high school. Clubs and summer programs appealed to our entrepreneurial side, giving us the chance to build our own projects and business ideas. It was in our coursework too. Entrepreneurship was a fairly popular class that I took my senior year, where our capstone project was to write up a business plan about a unique idea we had. Many of my high school classmates began their own entrepreneurial ventures, oftentimes teaming up with other students, and have had a good amount of success.

We, as a generation, are finding unique opportunities to leverage technology in entrepreneurial ventures. Take Peter Szabo, for instance, a twenty-one-year-old Slovakian Gen Zer who began to learn the ins-and-outs of Facebook marketing at eleven years old. Now, he manages millions of dollars of clients' Facebook advertising assets.[9]

In a nutshell, entrepreneurship is relatively blind of age. We hear about young entrepreneurs creating cool businesses, and it's empowering. Regardless of education or background, anyone with a good idea and strong work ethic can build a viable business from the ground up. Even

9   "Peter Szabo," 2019.

though some research suggests that older individuals with industry experience may make for better entrepreneurs,[10] time and time again, especially in the world of tech, we see young entrepreneurs succeeding. As Facebook CEO Mark Zuckerberg said, "Young people are just smarter." Whether that's true or not isn't relevant, but it goes to show that age discrimination, at least toward younger people, is breaking down.

Once I entered college, an emphasis on entrepreneurship grew larger. At Duke, many students are involved with start-ups on campus, and there are many resources at the school supporting student entrepreneurs, such as coursework in entrepreneurship and competitions that provide seed money for new business ideas. It's not just limited to wealthier private universities. Wake Tech, a local community college, has partnered with Wells Fargo to launch the Center for Entrepreneurship, providing hundreds of students with training on starting and growing a business. There's definitely a strong allure of entrepreneurship, and it's growing.

And why is that? Yes, schools and the world around us have placed a bigger emphasis on entrepreneurship, but that's more of an *effect* of us having a greater interest in entrepreneurship rather than a *cause* for our interest. Starting

---

10 "The 9th Annual State Of Entrepreneurship Address," 2018, *Ewing Marion Kauffman Foundation.*

businesses isn't a new concept—humans have been making business transactions for as long as we've been on this planet. Part of it has to do with greater media exposure and an uptick in books, articles, and movies made about every facet of entrepreneurship imaginable,[11] but a huge component has to do with an enormous interest in entrepreneurship by newer generations, millennials and Gen Z.

This interest is due to a variety of factors. A big part of it has to do with control of our financial futures. As we'll explore in later chapters, Gen Zers are very practical when it comes to money. When the recession hit, we saw and learned how fickle the economy can be and how difficult it was for people to get back into their pre-recession lifestyles, if they ever did. Entrepreneurship, while inherently risky, gives us a sense of control of our financial futures.

In a typical large corporation, even if we put in a lot of time and effort, there's the fear that we could be laid off at any moment. And yes, startups fail very often, but the owner feels a sense of control over his or her business's future that's missing when working in a big company. Plus, entrepreneurship is romanticized as something fueled by hard work and grit, which appeals greatly to hardworking Gen Zers.

---

11 "Media Attention For Entrepreneurship," *The World Bank*.

Another factor is just how much opportunity there is in today's world for new businesses to pop up. We've grown up surrounded by technology, and in the past, tech has been a shining beacon of opportunity for hopeful entrepreneurs. We realize the world isn't perfect and see a lot of potential to spark change. With the youngest members of our generation just starting to enter elementary school, this technological growth will snowball as older members of Gen Z pave the way with new technological advancements for younger members to then build upon.

And I think the largest reasons have to do with a distinct mindset shift on the sacrifices needed to start a business. Why risk it all on a venture that might collapse without having something to fall back on? Gen Zers don't view entrepreneurship as a career-encompassing path, but more of a "side hustle" that can be explored while completing school or working full-time. An entrepreneur could work full-time during the day and then work on building a startup in the evening and weekends.

I talked to a good friend of mine, James Arnold, who started a business called Scholarship Landscaping in the tenth grade. A lot of students mow lawns as a way to make quick income, but James went a step further and built a small business to address the lack of larger-scale landscaping project work in the community. We went to high school together and now we're both in the same college, so I've seen his company grow over time.

"We specialize in project-based landscaping work, and the reason is so I can easily shift my workload up and down," said James. He emphasizes the flexibility of the job above all else. "I really like to be able to pick my hours. If it gets busy at school, I can [scale back] if I need to." He hires part-time workers during busier times when taking on larger projects.

And it's been very rewarding. "Originally, I was trying to get some fun money to use on the side, to go out with friends, watch movies, do whatever," when referring to the mowing he did for neighbors in middle school before starting his business. "And then, once it became an official business, I shifted toward saving for college. College costs a lot of money," he says with a laugh.

Starting up a business gave James control over his financial future, as he could set his own hours depending on availability and how much money he needed. And he capitalized on the skills he gained through running a business, specifically management and communication. "I feel like [I've gotten] a lot more out of this than bagging groceries or running a cash register or something."

A key point here is that James doesn't want to work in landscaping post-graduation. He's pursuing a double major in electrical/computer engineering and computer science. He says that he isn't entirely sure what he wants to do in the future, but entrepreneurship is definitely an option—if there's a cool opportunity, he'll go for it.

For James, his business was not a life-encompassing career, but more of a side project that gave him good income and something fun to build and nurture. And Gen Zers love their side projects. Given the rapid growth of the gig economy, many Gen Zers take up a long-term hobby/freelance gig, from professional photography to blogging, designing websites to reselling clothes. Studies estimate that between 35 percent[12] and 48 percent[13] of adult Gen Zers are freelancers, a number that's expected to continue growing in the coming years.

I see it everywhere. Tons of students are involved in media production and photography, running social media pages for startups and building websites, to name a few. In a sense, and this is a bit meta, me writing this book is an example of a side project. Most of the year, I'm either in school or working full-time, and so writing is definitely a side job for me—I set

---

12 "35% Of The U.S. Workforce Is Now Freelancing—10 Million More Than 5 Years Ago," 2019, *Fast Company*.
13 "Freelancing In America: 2019 Survey - Upwork," 2019, *upwork.com*.

aside time every day to do research, set up or take interviews, and jot my ideas down. Overall, for entrepreneurial work, there's an allure in choosing your own work, setting your own rates and hours, having multiple income streams, and essentially being your own boss. And, as we'll talk about in more detail later on, it's incredibly empowering to know that you're solving an issue and making an impact on others.

When I first began digging into Gen Z views on entrepreneurship, I found very conflicting research. Some said that because Gen Zers are more practical, they'll ignore entrepreneurship, and others similarly published results that claimed Gen Zers were less eager to become entrepreneurs. But a key detail was phrasing: typically, when Gen Zers were asked whether they'd rather pursue entrepreneurship or go to the workforce, the number saying they wanted to become entrepreneurs was quite low. But when it wasn't phrased as an either/or question, implying that one didn't necessarily have to give up a regular job to be an entrepreneur, numbers were much higher.

Some will forgo "traditional" work entirely, making enough of a living to do 100 percent freelance work rather than working a nine to five. Others will choose to have side work or side jobs along with their full-time jobs. This is one way Gen Zers are similar to millennials. Both generations love freelance work, Gen Zers more so because we're still in school and can spend time to hone skills we know we'll need in the future.

At this point, you may be asking yourself, "Well, if Gen Zers want to go and start their own businesses or do freelance work, how does that help existing businesses?" Yes, Gen Zers are becoming increasingly interested in entrepreneurship and freelance work, but it's not a big reason to be alarmed.

Entrepreneurial Gen Zers help businesses tremendously because they can apply that same innovative mindset to drive business internally. Not all people with entrepreneurial qualities will create (or try to create) a successful business, and so many of these people will go to industry. A commonly used term nowadays sums it up: "intrapreneurship."

Richard Branson, founder of the Virgin Group, wrote a lot to say on the matter. "While it's true that every company needs an entrepreneur to get it under way, healthy growth requires a smattering of intrapreneurs who drive new projects and explore new and unexpected directions for business development. Virgin could never have grown into the group of more than 200 companies it is now, were it not for a steady stream of intrapreneurs who looked for and developed opportunities, often leading efforts that went against the grain."[14]

---

14   Richard Branson, 2019, "Richard Branson On Intrapreneurs," *msnbc.com*.

"[Gen Z] is looking at the world through a different lens, they're looking at the world not in terms of, 'I have a job to do, and I just need to do it,' but 'I have a job to do, and is there a better way to do it?'" said Court Lorenzini when speaking to me about his observations on entrepreneurial Gen Zers. He's a serial entrepreneur and a founder of Docu-Sign. Today, he works extensively with early stage entrepreneurs, especially on Duke's campus, to help them succeed. "You could have this mentality as an artist, as a janitor, as a doctor, as an attorney." Someone could be an intrapreneur without having gone through the typical entrepreneurial route earlier in life.

To be clear, it's not that only a few individuals have any entrepreneurial ability or, to a greater extent, creativity. Everyone exhibits these qualities. But Gen Z, due to the emphasis on entrepreneurship we've experienced throughout our lives, have these innovative qualities in spades and are already making huge waves.

Because of this, attracting new talent is more important than ever. "The more we foster [entrepreneurial] behavior, at every level . . . no matter whether they're startups or big companies, we're going to have more successful employees, we're going to have happier people, and we're going to have more efficient operations," said Lorenzini.

This becomes doubly important when considering competition. If Competitor X succeeds in hiring a ton of new, innovative graduates, they'll have a strong advantage. One big, and admittedly difficult, change can be to foster a startup-like environment. If you work for or own a small business or startup, this should be pretty easy. Gen Zers will gravitate toward small businesses they share similar values and vision with, especially those that prioritize being receptive to new hires' ideas and feedback. If you're at a larger company, this can be much more difficult to establish. Rigid hierarchy and corporate politics block this startup culture.

What I'm suggesting isn't new; large companies are constantly trying to find ways to spark change within the workplace to trigger the same kind of growth mentality startups have. To be clear, fostering a startup environment is not merely about adding a ping pong table or kombucha station, but rather having a clear, transparent vision for the future and encouraging a growth mindset both in the company and in employees. That means having the ambition to say, "This is where we want our company in five years," and also being able to say, "If the company grows, you, the employee, will grow with us." Ultimately, it means tying the employee to a company's journey and making sure that employee knows he or she was a pivotal part of that journey.

Some large companies have already achieved this. Take Tesla, for instance. Despite having a (supposedly) incredibly stressful working environment filled with short deadlines and numerous safety incidents, it's one of the most sought after companies to work for right now, in large part due to a commitment toward innovation and sparking change in a relatively stagnant industry.

Innovative people gravitate toward innovative companies. It's Newton's second law. This is especially important for Gen Zers, because not only will innovative and entrepreneurial Gen Z employees head to these companies, they'll also say to their friends, "Yeah, I absolutely love working at *Company Name*. You should send in a resume—I'll refer you!" Word-of-mouth has always been powerful, but it is even more relevant now due to the power of the Internet. Instead of simply saying, "Look at this company," we can now write up an email with the company's website, Glassdoor reviews, location, and open positions in a neat little paragraph to send to a friend.

Let's focus on the actual side work itself in a professional environment. A lot of employers frown upon moonlighting (having another job in addition to one's primary employment). Some explicitly ban side businesses, while others are very wary due to the potential for a conflict of interest, such as having a business in the same field and potentially sharing trade secrets, a drop in productivity, or use of company time and resources for the business.

This same mentality will do more harm than good in future years unless some changes are made. As stated earlier, nearly half of current adult Gen Zers have freelance gigs on the side. From a firsthand perspective, a lot of my friends in school say that they intend to work full-time but also have passions that they'd like to pursue on the side, whether as hobbies or additional work. So, having strict anti-moonlighting policies in place will turn away a lot of talented Gen Zers, simply because of how popular side work is becoming.

Allowing employees to have their own side projects, freelance work, and businesses should be the norm. Many people, Gen Zers included, approach their side work with a high level of professionalism and will strive to keep this work from interfering with their full-time jobs. Here's an idea: rather than blocking moonlighting from the get-go, have policies that state that side work is a privilege, and if it interferes with work at the company, they can be subject to whatever punishment the company decides. This deterrence will stop most from actively thinking or working on other projects while at their primary job, while still allowing the freedom to pursue passions or extra income as soon as they clock out.

Gen Z is the most entrepreneurial—and innovative—generation in history. And while not all Gen Zers have aspirations of launching sports cars into outer space, we are full of creativity that, when nurtured, can lead to bold new ideas and a renewed sense of purpose for a company.

Key Takeaways:

- Gen Zers love entrepreneurship and side freelance work: Almost half of adult Gen Zers have a freelance gig, and that number is expected to rise. Entrepreneurship gives us a path to pursue passions, have side income streams, teach us valuable skills, and create our own hours.

- Intrapreneurship: We are the most innovative generation in history, and that innovation can be a huge benefit for companies. When individuals are creative and take the initiative to pursue new potential solutions, they can generate massive returns for a company.

- Attracting Gen Z may require radical changes: We crave a workplace that appeals to our entrepreneurial side and has a strong growth mindset. When businesses don't have a clear vision for the future, both in terms of where a company is going and where they want to take employees, innovative Gen Zers are turned away. Through respecting our desire for side gigs and really hammering home that the company is going places, resumes will pile up.

DIGITAL NATIVES

———

"Don't mess around with the iPad," said my dad. "I need to set it up first."

My little brother and I nodded. As soon as my dad left the room, we went to work.

When my dad returned after taking a call, my brother and I were taking turns playing a racing simulator on the iPad. In the half hour he was away, we had configured the iPad, changed the wallpaper, and downloaded a handful of apps. He was pretty surprised.

I was eleven at the time, and my brother was seven. Truthfully, my brother did most of the work setting it up, while I lazily recommended apps to download. And though Apple devices aren't too difficult to configure, looking back, it was still a pretty impressive task for us to accomplish.

Nowadays, kids are even more tech-savvy. Toddlers handle phones, tablets, and laptops with ease—I still remember my little cousin, three years old at the time, navigating You-Tube to find toy review videos. We Gen Zers are true digital natives, fully incorporating technology with our everyday lives.

If you've ever been around Gen Zers, you know how much we like gadgets. You know the stereotypes: all we want to do is stare at our screens and tap out meaningless texts, scroll mindlessly through social media, and play online pool. I'd like to paint a more comprehensive picture. It's true that we have grown accustomed to and rely on tech, but this has both pros and cons that will greatly shape how we influence and are influenced by the workplace.

First, a distinction: When it comes to growing up with technology, people like to lump millennials and Gen Zers together. After all, both generations are supposedly screen-obsessed. But there's a fundamental difference between both groups. Millennials grew up as the tech boom began, never experiencing smartphones or social media as children. They explored the Internet in its infancy, tinkering with dial-up modems and AOL chatrooms, and watched it evolve into the cornerstone of worldwide commerce, entertainment, and communication it is today. And as such, they had an intrinsic fascination with new technology that continues to this date.

Gen Zers, on the other hand, have grown up in the midst of the tech boom. Ever since we can remember, we've been surrounded by technology. For reference, I'm on the upper end age-wise of Gen Z, and barely recall a few once cutting-edge technologies. I remember a teacher showing me an archaic floppy disk once in elementary school and from then on, we used flash drives and eventually the cloud. Even in elementary school, I remember a few of my friends getting their first phones, which were iPhones.

Throughout our lives, we've been plugged in. Therefore, as a whole, we're less fazed by new technology entering the market, less wowed by the coolness factor of a product and more interested in its long-term benefits. Simply put, new technology isn't much of a novelty for us, but more of a tool to connect with others, entertain us, and aid us in our daily lives.

Because of this, a very interesting trend develops. We use and love tech, but still prefer to talk to people in-person in the workplace. In fact, a study found that 53 percent of Gen Zers prefer face-to-face communication over tech-heavy forms of communication like email, video conferencing, and instant messaging.[15] A live poll held at a conference for Gen Zers showed that 72 percent preferred face-to-face communication at work.[16]

As a generation, we still prefer digital communication outside of the workplace, just because of how easy it is to communicate with someone who isn't nearby. It makes much more sense to send a text or direct message to a friend rather than flagging them down in public. But when everyone is crammed in the same building at work, this distance barrier is removed.

Maybe all those times we've heard "get off your phone" is actually having an impact. Based on interactions with friends, it seems like there's a bit of a countermovement nowadays against constantly being glued to screens. In college, for instance, it seems like there's a social urge to head outside rather than sit on a laptop all day. "You've been in your room all afternoon studying, let's grab some dinner." We recognize how addicting tech is and try to avoid it when there's better things to do.

---

15 Dan Schawbel, 2019, "Gen Y And Gen Z Global Workplace Expectations Study," *millennialbranding.com*.

16 Jenkins, Ryan, 2019, "This Is How Generation Z Will Communicate At Work," *Inc.*.

For instance, my friends and I like to play the phone stacking game. When we go out to dinner, we all put our phones and other devices in a big stack on the corner of the table and turn off Do Not Disturb mode. Traditionally, the game is played where whoever caves first and picks up their phone has to pay for everyone's food. Since my friends and I are all broke, we choose different punishments rather than one big wallet-draining payment. It's fun in a chaotic way—throughout the meal, there'll be various chimes, rings, vibrations, and more emanating from the phone pile. We're all risking missed calls from Mom, but it's a pretty fun way to curb our tech obsession, at least for a short while.

A major point missed by most mainstream media reporting on "digital slaves" (aka Gen Zers) is that we are very aware of our increased use of tech. We are deeply aware of the pros and cons of technology use, especially social media.

"We live in this world with so much new technology, and our future is going to have a lot of technology. It's different from what adults grew up with, but that doesn't necessarily mean it's worse. It just means we need to tackle this change thoughtfully," said a high schooler that My Digital Tat2, a non-profit organization that "helps young people think critically about their power and responsibility in a connected world," interviewed.[17]

This is why I criticize "Gen Z experts" who aren't Gen Zers themselves. They love to insult young people for being glued to their phones (even if these same people are on Facebook for hours a day), but there are a lot of benefits to technology use. I don't want to call out anyone in particular (other than Jean Twenge) but through building the false idea that young people's tech use is making us lazy and unprepared, older generations are less receptive to our needs and wants and less willing to foster effective use of innovative technology solutions that new employees can use to boost productivity.

With that being said, we like technology because of how useful it is. We leverage it for easy entertainment, communication, and networking (after all, writing this book, from conducting research to contacting experts for interviews, would have been a lot more difficult without a thorough understanding of how to use the internet). But because we recognize how easy it is to get sucked into the digital world, we aren't as eager to adopt the newest and flashiest technology as older generations seem to think.

---

17 Gloria Moskowitz-Sweet and Erica Pelavin, 2019, "Generation Z Is Far More Nuanced About Tech Than Its Predecessors," *Pacific Standard.*

So what does this mean? Yes, Gen Zers love tech and they want to see tech incorporated in the workplace, but this tech needs to have a purpose. New communication software like Slack, Yammer, and even companies' custom-built internal messaging systems are used to facilitate a flood of instant messages within a company. This instant messaging is quick and virtually effortless, appealing to millennials. But, as mentioned, Gen Zers want a human factor in the work they do. Personally, if I have a question or comment for someone close by in the workplace, I'd much rather walk over to them and talk—beyond stretching out my legs, it enables me to have more effective communication than a simple IM or email, and shows that I care about whatever I had to say.

At a business, implementing new communication technology such as Slack is a good idea for those who want to use it, but there's no need to push for widescale adoption of this technology. Given our generation's growing preference to talk face-to-face when we're able to (such as when working three cubicles away from a coworker) encouraging the use of instant messaging software could be counterintuitive, especially given how much of our day is spent slogging through emails and other messages anyways.

So far, I've been talking about communication through tech exclusively, but technology is more than just chatting. A key way we use tech is as a means to an end, a way to improve our daily lives. Need to go to a friend's house but don't have a car handy? Hail an Uber. Want to spellcheck that important essay? Paste it into Grammarly. It's reached a point where we can even ask Alexa to add groceries to a shopping list, which can then be purchased and shipped with a click of a button. It saves us the hassle of adding items manually on a computer or *gasp* going to a grocery store ourselves.

Just look at Amazon Prime. It promises two-day shipping, something unheard of just a mere decade ago. And they're experimenting with shortening that timeframe to one day or less using better distribution logistics. According to their website, they hope to roll out drones soon that can deliver lightweight packages in under thirty minutes, perfect for when you're scrambling for that last-minute gift for your significant other.

This is why we Gen Zers like tech so much: it makes life easier. Call us lazy, but because we've grown up while these new, time-saving, and productivity-boosting tools were being developed, we've learned to leverage them in our daily lives.

I'll give an example: Gen Z, more than any other generation, is shunning cash,[18] and when possible, credit and debit cards too. On campus, I never carry my wallet around, because I

18   "What Gen Z Thinks About Payments," 2019, *Seeking Alpha.*

can slap my smartphone onto a scanner to pay for things. The entire process only takes a second, maybe two or three if I'm fishing around for my phone.

On top of that, apps like Venmo and the Cash App make it easy to send money to friends. If I'm having dinner with a couple of friends and (like typical students) we agree to pay for our own purchases, rather than asking the waiter or waitress for separate checks, one person will pay for everyone and we'll all Venmo that person later.

By making purchases on my password-protected phone, I save time, don't have to carry a bulky wallet, and reduce my possibility of getting mugged. A win-win-win.

But there are other things motivating our love of technology. Businesses love to throw around terms like "the future of work," and we Gen Zers are receptive of this. Rapid technology change underpins many fears over what the future holds, typically due to automation and oft-mentioned "AI." This doesn't mean *everyone* wants to study computer science, even if many Gen Zers are doing so. But at the very least, it means that we're open to new possibilities through tech.

Social media, which we'll look at in more depth in the next chapter, has ushered in a massive, new way of marketing, and Gen Zers have capitalized on this huge opportunity.

Between vlogging (aka video blogging), comedy sketches, and fashion reviews, social media stars have picked up on just about every facet of entertainment. And when you break it down, it's pretty cool. Social media stars, many of whom are still in high school, have found a way to capitalize on a topic that fascinates them, building up huge followings and finding ways to monetize their success in many ways, from product placement to advertisements and testimonials. And these skills are hugely transferable. It's not just being able to say, "Hey, I'm good at social media, maybe I can help companies with theirs," but also having the technical know-how to create quality content, amass interest, leverage different platforms and tools, and create entertainment value. And it's a job that didn't exist twenty years ago.

"I think a lot of the Gen Z applicants already have completely transferable skills. They've got their own following and their own power base. So, it's no longer guessing based on credentials around for where you went to school. It's what people are currently doing," said Aaron Paquette, the career market researcher who specializes in media and entertainment that I introduced in the first chapter. "[In the past], if you wanted to big media career, it was all about interviewing at CBS . . . now a lot of the Gen Z folks who want to be media already have feeds and are already producing content."

Granted, not everyone is a social media star (I'm certainly not). But this is just one way we're exploring what new technology has to offer. Having been on the internet all our lives, we've grown accustomed to learning new pieces of software and becoming experts without even knowing it. Many of my friends are skilled in Adobe Photoshop and have never taken a course to learn it. Others flock to free massive online open courses (MOOCs) led by top university professors to learn practical skills for the future. YouTube tutorials and trial-and-error are enough to lead us to success, and we've adopted a do-it-yourself mentality for learning and applying new things.

There are many numbers thrown around regarding the future of work. Some say 85 percent of jobs that will exist in 2030 haven't been invented yet, while others are more conservative at 65 percent or less.[19] Still, these are pretty large numbers, and many of these envisioned jobs for the future—like a drone manager or a human-technology integration specialist (essentially an IT manager on steroids)—are heavily based in technology.

We like technology in the workplace because it enables new ways of tackling problems and making us more productive. Imagine if your company stored the majority of files

---

19 "Realizing 2030: A Divided Vision Of The Future," 2019, *Dell Technologies Inc.*.

in manila folders instead of electronically (hopefully you don't use paper data storage in this day and age). Sure, there would be growing pains to adopting electronic file storage, but the pros would greatly outweigh the cons. Similarly, as new technologies are being developed today, Gen Zers want to see companies being proactive about at least trying out these technologies, because we see technology as the key to the future.

Key Takeaways:

- Gen Zers are true digital natives: We've grown up during a massive boom in technology, and our phones and tablets have become extra limbs for us. We are always plugged in, and while recognizing that there are drawbacks to this, we view our connection to technology as an overall benefit.

- But we still like face-to-face communication: When far from each other, digital communication obviously reigns supreme. But in the workplace, Gen Zers prefer communicating in-person. The reasons are many, from a desire to communicate thoughts more clearly than a simple "K" via text, to simply wanting to make daily life at work more personable. There's been a push toward increasing digital communication in the workplace in recent years, but this might just add to the "email overload" problem and cause Gen Zers to be glued to cubicles.

- We want to see *meaningful* technology: If I had a choice between having a big, flashy TV on the wall where I work or a laptop upgrade to load apps faster, I'd choose the laptop upgrade in a heartbeat. Gen Zers are multitaskers and want to see technology that makes life easier. On a basic level, this could mean software that saves time or presentation technology that makes business meetings more engaging.

SOCIAL MEDIA IN
THE WORKPLACE

It's a warm, sunny day on Duke University's campus. As I walk to my next class, a student is setting up her DSLR camera, preparing for a photoshoot in front of a huge oak tree. Students and parents touring the campus snap selfies on their smartphones. I pull out my phone and take a picture of the trees lining the sidewalk. Within seconds, I apply a Snapchat filter that simply says "Durham," and send it off to a friend.

We are infatuated with photography. It is a hobby that is easy to enter—anyone with a smartphone can capture the world around them. Unlike painting or sculpting, which require tremendous amounts of time and effort, taking a photo is as simple as pointing and clicking.

But it also has a large learning curve. As soon as someone decides to take the plunge into photography, they're bombarded with technical jargon: aperture, exposure, ISO, RAW files. It offers enough of a challenge to be a thrilling hobby.

But one thing that makes photography, and media as a whole, so relevant now is the popularity of social media. Gen Zers spend approximately three hours a day on social media. It's seeped into every aspect of our lives. We wake up scrolling through Twitter and go to bed watching YouTube and sending DMs.[20]

Walk through any high school cafeteria and you'll find dozens of students scrolling away on their phones, liking, following, tweeting, and posting away when they aren't chatting with people around them. The amount of raw information we can convey with just a few pictures is unlike anything we've seen before. Within seconds of opening Instagram, you can see an update on your friend's weekend trip to the beach, news about an upcoming political march, and an ad for your favorite apparel brand. Through photos and videos, we are able to convey feeling and emotion, and capture soon-to-be memories.

---

20 Katie Young, 2018, "3 Ways Gen Z And Millennials Use Social Media Differently - Globalwebindex Blog."

They say a picture is worth a thousand words, and I definitely agree. People would much rather share a few photos or videos than write thousands of words (a bit ironic, since I'm writing a book). The point is that social media makes the spread of information seamless and instant, revolutionizing how we spread and take in information.

The purpose of this chapter, and the book as a whole, isn't to talk about product marketing for Gen Z. There's already a ton of research on using social media to attract Gen Z consumers and creating effective marketing plans for the biggest generation in the world. But there's much less written about what Gen Zers are looking for in employers and how to leverage social media in the workplace. This is where I'll focus this chapter: why is our social media obsession a good thing, both in recruitment and while working at a company?

Social media is powerful. By one estimate, when people hear a statistic or fact, they're only 10 percent likely to remember that information three days later. But when that same information is paired with a relevant image, they are 65 percent likely to remember.[21]

---

21   John Medina, 2019, "Vision | Brain Rules |," *brainrules.net.*

This is a picture of a dog wearing sunglasses.[22] It has nothing to do with the content of this chapter (unfortunately). Most

---

22   Alan King, 2017, *Brown Dog Photo*, Image.

readers would look at this dog as soon as they flip the page, showing how our eyes are naturally drawn to entertaining images over text. And given the statistic above, if you only remember a few things from this book, this picture will likely be one of them.

Think about what social media websites and apps do. They provide thousands of images, videos, and other forms of content that are easily navigable and appeal to our generation's supposed eight-second attention span. Gen Z isn't hooked on social media consumption simply to like our friends' posts and look at memes. We realize how effective it is in communicating and sharing information. Gen Zers who realized how powerful social media is have been propelled into stardom. As I mentioned in the previous chapter, platforms like YouTube, Vine, Facebook, TikTok, and Instagram are perfect for creating and promoting just about any content imaginable. Social media influencers are everywhere, some earning seven figures and becoming famous in a particular niche industry, from modeling to gaming, cooking to comedy.

That being said, Gen Zers are excellent social media managers and have many years of experience under their belts. A lot of my friends do part-time work managing small businesses' social media pages, earning decent money while rapidly growing their company's social media footprint. It's an easy job—they'll be sitting in class while rapidly but strategically liking, commenting, and following members of their target audience to boost the brand's visibility.

From a technical standpoint, many Gen Zers are savvy in photo editing and manipulation—the vast majority have experience in light photo retouching through the use of filters, and a growing proportion are growing comfortable with editing software such as Final Cut Pro and Blender.

And because we are digital natives, Gen Zers flit between new software and technologies quickly, picking up new knowledge fast. For the most part, unless the learning curve is very high and requires specialized training, learning a new piece of technology is as simple as watching tutorials and experimenting. If you're a small business or even a larger company looking to leverage newer social media platforms, hiring a Gen Zer part-time may have a huge return on investment.

Now let's focus on hiring Gen Zers in the first place. Search engines, word-of-mouth, and social media are primarily how we find jobs. This is true for millennials, and it'll be true for Gen Z as well. Sure, at the senior level, headhunters do a lot of recruiting, but for entry-level positions, Gen Zers are going to use these same methods.

Let's break each of these down. Search engines are pretty straightforward. When scribbling down a list of places to apply to, the simplest method is to simply Google a job description and maybe a location. From there, potential jobs can be narrowed down based on experience and skills. Not much to say in this regard, other than Google and more niche sites for job seeking like Indeed and Monster are doing a pretty great job. For Gen Z, traditional search engines work excellently for getting that first inkling on where to apply.

Word-of-mouth in applying for jobs is extremely popular among Gen Z. To understand why, let's draw a comparison. I know I promised not to talk about marketing to Gen Z, but bear with me. When shopping, Gen Zers love reviews. Eighty-six percent of Gen Zers read reviews before making a purchase, far more than any other generation.[23] Personally, if I see an ad for something cool on Instagram, rather than just hitting buy or putting it on a wish list, I immediately look to the comments to see if many people are saying it's not worth the money. From there, since companies can delete negative comments from their ads, I google the product for further reviews. The majority of the time, I don't end up making a purchase, despite how hyper-targeted Instagram's algorithms are to my shopping tastes. But if reviews are stellar, I'll buy.

Word-of-mouth is the equivalent to online reviews when it comes to job searching. If we can have a candid talk with

---

23 "Annual Gen Z Research Studies – Trends, Stats, Attitudes & More," 2019, *The Center For Generational Kinetics*.

someone at the company we're talking to, our interest is piqued. Even if it's a well-known company like Google or Goldman Sachs, students ask their friends who intern or work there what they think of the experience and how much they like the work they do. It's all about finding a fit. Yes, there are trends with Gen Z, and analyzing these trends is the purpose of this book, but ultimately, each person is different and has their own preferences for what makes a job fulfilling, achieves work-life balance, etc. Word-of-mouth doesn't have to be a literal face-to-face discussion. Messages online work just as well, along with job review sites (like Glassdoor) and indirect word-of-mouth recommendations. For instance, saying to someone, "My friend worked for Company Y, and he really liked it."

Social media is the most unique and powerful way Gen Zers find and get jobs. We flock to platforms built upon professional networking and job hunting. LinkedIn, for instance, has made it incredibly easy to build and grow our networks. Everyone we know is in one neat and organized place, and we can easily reach out to people we don't know yet through mutual connections.

If I hear about a job or internship that piques my interest, I search for the company on LinkedIn and learn as much as I can. And because LinkedIn is a social platform, one of my main priorities is seeing if anyone from my network or any alumni from my school who worked there. From there, the word-of-mouth component comes into play, and I reach out to employees to get a feel for what the company is like.

But it's not just LinkedIn that's used for a job search. Gen Zers want to work for companies whose values resonate with them, and other social media platforms are even better at facilitating this search. If your company has a sizable social media presence, kudos to you. But how you approach social media is incredibly important. Take, for instance, a company that sells makeup products. Already, a lot of Gen Zers might be following your brand, but they're interested as consumers rather than potential employees. Instead of simply promoting products and hiring influencers, offer a glimpse into the lives of employees there. Between sharing employee volunteering days, spotlights on hardworking employees, social initiatives your company is passionate about, and more, viewers will feel a pull toward a company.

Top tech companies, for instance, are seeing record levels of applications from young employees, despite being compared to monopolies and experiencing recent privacy scandals. A big chunk of it has to do with the fact that Gen Zers like tech and want to work for tech companies that pay well, but big tech also seems to be very socially aware. For instance, companies like Google and Microsoft offer competitive scholarships and internships for underrepresented minorities. Companies are essentially telling the world that they are trying to make their workplaces more welcoming and inclusive. The funny part is that these companies are still largely made up of white males, but by showing that they're making an effort to be more diverse through social media platforms and the news, Gen Z is being pulled toward them. (Note: there's been a lot of criticism about whether companies are making a genuine push for diversity or whether it's more for show. It's something we'll explore in later chapters. If companies fail to actually create a more diverse workplace, there will likely be backlash.)

So, leveraging social media is huge for new employees. It doesn't matter if you're a recruiter or not; tools like LinkedIn have made it easy for anyone in the company to reach out to an ideal candidate and offer insight on what it's like to work there. Craft a brand image that resonates with Gen Zers, such as showing how a once entry-level employee progressed to top management or social initiatives that the company is spearheading. Social media can be as proactive as you want it to be, and ultimately, the companies that leverage social media platforms well will attract top talent.

There's also the burning question of how social media can be used *within* the company. So you've hired a supposed so-cial-media obsessed Gen Zer. Now what?

"While 72 percent of companies use social technologies in some way, very few are anywhere near to achieving the full potential benefit. In fact, the most powerful applications of social technologies in the global economy are largely untapped," wrote the McKinsey Global Institute.[24] "By fully implementing social technologies, companies have an opportunity to raise the productivity of interaction workers—high-skill knowledge workers, including managers and professionals—by 20 to 25 percent."

For one, social media is built for collaboration. When you want to validate an idea, social media is a great way to address an audience that'll listen. For instance, if an employee is tasked with making an app and the project isn't under wraps, he may ask his Twitter following for advice. "Does this user interface look solid?" "Should I add this feature?" Social media is an excellent way to connect with experts in a field and gain valuable input.

Here's another example. If you've dabbled in programming, then you definitely know about Stack Overflow. It's a massive forum for programmers to post and answer specific coding questions and has revolutionized the industry. Rather than having to crack open a textbook or take a long, thought-provoking shower, we can browse the site for help. And if we

---

24 "The Social Economy: Unlocking Value And Productivity Through Social Technologies," 2012, *McKinsey & Company.*

don't see a similar question already posted on the site, we can post our own questions and have them answered within hours. Whether trying to self-teach yourself a programming language or trying to debug a complex chunk of code, you can rely on millions of supportive Stack Overflow users.

Despite being branded as a Q&A site, Stack Overflow is a social network. It allows experts in certain disciplines of computer science to gain fame within the platform, and many tech companies reach out to top contributors on Stack Overflow for their hiring needs. And it's created a buzzing community that facilitates a tremendous amount of collaboration with people who would otherwise be strangers.

Social media is also very valuable in market research, and not just polls and surveys—that can be done with an email list. But, for instance, you could tease a picture of a future product to assess excitement. Social media analytics have gotten so detailed and accurate that you can easily pinpoint which ideas are really buzzing and which ones are flops among consumers. This is especially relevant for smaller companies without dedicated marketing and social outreach teams. Given our native understanding of social media, Gen Z is perfectly poised to lead marketing and research initiatives for companies and leverage new technologies in creative ways that haven't been explored yet.

Within the workplace, especially at larger companies, social media is very valuable in keeping the business connected. Through social media platforms, including rudimentary blogs and forums proprietary to a company, different departments can gain a grander picture of a company's vision for the future and how different departments' work aid the company in achieving this vision. Facilitating this interconnectedness can help employees see how their work fits into the bigger picture of the company.

And (for lack of a better term) social media is honest, mainly because of how easy it is for a community of users to tear apart a public post. For instance, if a company posts an altered statistic, even if 99 percent of followers don't notice anything, a few people might, and that's all it takes for credibility to come crumbling down. In an era of distrust in big institutions, consumers are expecting greater transparency with companies in order to regain trust. 81 percent of people believe social media has increased accountability for businesses[25] because we view social media as a window into what companies value and how genuinely committed they are toward improving society. However, it's important to note that this statistic is for *all* Americans, not just Gen Zers, as research on Gen Z's level of trust in big institutions is still inconclusive. This detail is important because companies and

25 "#Brandsgetreal: Social Media & The Evolution Of Transparency," 2019, *Sprout Social.*

governments love to tote that young people are much more distrustful of institutions, thereby shifting the blame from themselves to their critics and consumers.

Because we seek a level of candor with businesses, the opposite applies as well. If a business uses social media for ideation by branching out to its followers, people feel far more attached to the brand. This can be explicit by saying, "Let us know your thoughts on X in the comments below," and less direct, such as responding to as many comments on a post as feasible, regardless of whether they are positive or negative—doing so further cements this feeling of authenticity. Traditionally, research and development and social media marketing divisions are separate, with ideation solely in the hands of a few "idea people" in the company. But Gen Zers want to mesh them together and integrate the thoughts of the people with where companies should be heading. It's a tactic used by Gen Z entrepreneurs especially: instead of just offering a product or service to consumers, they make sure customers know that they are instrumental in the growth of the company.

All this goes to show that social media is poised to revolutionize the workplace, and Gen Z is its harbinger. At first glance, our addiction to social media seems to be a strong negative, but we've cultivated a unique skillset: the creation of likable and quality content, the ability to authentically promote, and being able to rapidly connect with a large audience of people who would otherwise be strangers. It's made us more connected, and we know how to create strategies to better engage other employees and our target consumers.

Key Takeaways:

- Gen Z loves taking photos and creating other forms of media: We're creators that want to make a big impact on the world. Our ability to make interesting, quality posts has launched many into stardom and has made us savants at creating sharable content. We recognize how powerful social media is and use it in every facet of our lives, from communication to entertainment, news to networking.

- Recruiting is changing: Gen Zers are skeptical by nature and want to see that a business is truly committed to whatever values they claim to follow. Creating an authentic company image is crucial to attracting top talent. Social media is also changing the way that applicants reach out to companies and vice versa. I'd estimate that at least half of all potential job opportunities I hear about are through social media platforms (the rest are mostly through talking with friends). Companies that don't recognize our love of social media and use it to proactively reach out to potential applicants will fall behind.

- Social media is powerful within the workplace: It opens up huge new possibilities for feedback simply because there are no barriers between the company and its target audience; simply open up Instagram and see who's following a company—those are your biggest fans. Gen Z is skilled in bouncing ideas off a company's target audience, enabling us to create prototypes and proof-of-concepts that closely resemble what customers say they want. It keeps employees connected and makes a company more approachable and authentic.

STABILITY

———

We watched the American Dream crumble.

I was eight when the Great Recession was in full swing. If you had asked me what was going on, the most I would have been able to say is, "The economy is doing bad." Despite this limited understanding of America's beaten down economy, I saw the effects firsthand: "For Sale" signs popping up around my neighborhood, friends and family losing their jobs, and charts plastered everywhere, all with downward sloping arrows. But above all else, I noticed a distinct atmosphere of fear and stress.

Classmates would talk about how their parents had lost their jobs, and I remember that even the teachers seemed stressed out. Because of overcrowding at my elementary school, my third grade classroom was in a trailer next to the main building (though truthfully, schools in the Raleigh area of North Carolina have never been able to keep up with growing student population).

The effects of the recession are still resonating all over the world. Many had their retirement savings wiped away and have had to work for many years longer than planned. Credit scores are rock bottom, and it's contributed to a significant wealth divide in America between whites and minority races.[26] Economists point to hysteresis, the Greek word for "scars," to explain how a crisis from over a decade ago caused, well, a scarring in the labor market.

During the Great Recession, everyone was focusing on adults, which obviously made sense since they were the ones worrying about foreclosures and arguing with brokers. But kids were largely overlooked and, well, we noticed things.

Granted, many Gen Zers don't have much of a recollection of the recession. They only remember the monumental post-recession expansion of the economy. But though the economy is going through record highs at the time of this writing, Gen Z can't shake off feelings of wariness, even fear, for the future.

---

26 Jennifer Streaks, 2018, "Black Families Have 10 Times Less Wealth Than Whites And The Gap Is Widening—Here's Why," *CNBC*.

A big part has to do with the sociopolitical environment of America and the world as a whole. Despite a strong economy, America's political climate isn't exactly rosy right now. We have a controversial figure in the White House and according to Deloitte, a general sense of distrust in a tight-lipped government.[27] There's also an intense fear of school shootings embedded in our minds. Top that off with a cutthroat race for top colleges, internships, and jobs, and older Gen Zers have a lot to worry about.

I talked with industrial and organizational psychologist Dr. Kenneth Matos, Lead People Scientist at Culture Amp, to gain further insight into what makes our generation less optimistic overall than the millennials before us.

"I like to describe the different generations in terms of whether or not they were a boom or bust generation." Boom generations, he explains, expect a lot of opportunity in the workplace, and that their success is directly influenced by how much effort they put in. "That very much describes the baby boomers. They're the children of the generation that fought in World War II, the Industrial Revolution transformed jobs, and people could be fairly confident that they could replicate the life that they anticipated."

27 "Deloitte Research Reveals A "Generation Disrupted": Growing Up In A World Of Accelerated Transformation Leaves Millennials And Gen Zs Feeling Unsettled About The Future," 2019, *Deloitte*.

Bust generations, on the other hand, don't expect an easy lifestyle. They feel that regardless of how hard they work, luck plays a huge role. "Gen X came of age in their own recession," says Matos, "and were pretty much disrespected by the generation before and labeled as slackers. There was a lot of under-investment in them, and general doubt in their value."

Interestingly, the older generations produced generations with similar mentalities. To rephrase, the children of baby boomers, millennials, also make up a boom generation. Similarly, the children of Gen X, Gen Zers, make up another bust generation.

It all boils down to how each generation was raised. Throughout their careers, baby boomers were rewarded with success if they put in enough hard work and dedication, and they raised their children with a similar attitude. Gen Xers didn't have the same outlook on life, and taught their children to work smarter rather than just harder and never expect that things will just "go our way."

So millennials began to enter the workforce, and they got screwed over by the Great Recession. Their optimism is now dissipating for many reasons, such as over $1.6 trillion of student loan debt, a volatile job market at the start of their careers, enormous rent payments, and a need to put off traditional stepping stones like marriage, raising kids, and buying homes. To top it all off, people have blamed millennials for these failures. As Michael Hobbs, senior enterprise reporter for HuffPost, writes, "According to The Olds, our problems are all our fault: We got the wrong degree. We spend money we don't have on things we don't need . . . Mention 'Millennial' to anyone over forty and the word 'entitlement' will come back at you within seconds, our own intergenerational game of Marco Polo."[28]

Gen Z noticed all this. Even though we've largely shaken off effects of The Great Recession and the economy is very strong, we saw how easy it was for that fragile sense of security to shatter for millennials. Though economic forecasting is beyond the scope of this book (and I know far too little to make any assertion), from a very simplified perspective, the economy has undergone its longest expansion ever on record. And this makes Gen Zers nervous, because we worry whether the economy, and job market, will stumble just as we enter the workforce. We are still optimistic for the future, but adopt a very, very practical mindset when preparing for it.

Overall, Gen Zers are focusing on practical decision making: how can we ensure our safety? How do we make ourselves as financially secure as possible?

---

28 Michael Hobbes, 2018, "Generation Screwed," *The Huffington Post.*

An example can be seen in a millennial trend toward buying experiences. The idea is that buying a product, like a nice car or flashy TV, only gives fleeting happiness and excitement. Numerous books and articles have been written saying that pursuing experiences, not things, is "the secret to happiness."

Don't get me wrong, Gen Zers love experiences too. But they're far less likely to drop a substantial amount of money into a trip or other experience.

For instance, imagine spending $7,000 on a backpacking trip through the Alps. It could be an amazing journey and make for awesome memories, but you're also short $7,000. It didn't have any financial rate of return at all. And so yes, you may be a little happier, something that millennials prioritize more than having a sturdy financial safety net, but lacking that $7,000 could cause extra stress down the road.

Many Gen Zers feel that the money could be better spent on something that ensures our future financial success, and that it's better to spend large when we have the means to.[29] For instance, it makes more sense for us to buy a nice house because it's a big, desirable purchase that we hope will appreciate in value over time. It's an important purchase with a noticeable ROI.

---

29 Janet Adamy, 2019, "Gen Z Is Coming To Your Office. Get Ready To Adapt.," *WSJ*.

Going back to the travel example, personally, whenever my friends and I go on short trips, we try to keep costs as low as possible while still having a blast. In May, I went to Myrtle Beach for three nights, splitting the costs with friends, and I spent less than $100 in total (minus food). Gen Zers do like fun experiences, but we're willing to hold off on expensive purchases that won't give our money back, at least until we feel financially comfortable enough to do so.

Gen Zers are known for their frugality and interest in long-term investing. When talking with a few of my friends, I noticed that many plan to save a significant portion of their income as soon as they start working, paying off debt as quickly as possible and putting the rest into investments. At least, so they claim—we all know how hard it is to save money. They're willing to live less-than-comfortably for a few years, avoiding big expenditures and renting cheap apartments. "Won't be worse than living in cramped dorms," mentioned my friend.

Compounding works its magic, and they'll have a comfortable nest egg amassed early in life. All-in-all, our generation is placing an emphasis on ensuring long-term safety and stability by seeking majors and jobs in high demand, planning to save money, and trying to avoid student debt.

There's more to safety than just financial safety, however. As a generation, we're more averse than previous generations to "risky" behaviors. Drug and alcohol use are less prominent,[30] teen birth rates have halved since 1991,[31] we're wearing Crocs,[32] and we fear that questionable behavior could be forever immortalized on the Internet. At the same time, however, mental health issues are becoming more prominent, something we'll explore in the next chapter.

Our desire for safety and a "what's in it for us" mentality aren't suddenly going to switch off once we enter the job market. Employers can do many things to appeal to our sense of practicality, and in doing so, can become more attractive in the eyes of our generation.

Apart from salary and expected workload commitment, when we're looking at jobs to join, we focus on benefits. But these benefits need to have a clear-cut impact for our futures. We want things along the lines of employer-matching 401k programs—the higher the match, the better. Dental and vision insurance are important, even pet insurance (Gen Z likes pets).[33] We ignore the "fluff," and see how our employers are going to take care of us.

---

30 Ibid.

31 "Decrease In Teen Pregnancy." 2019. *Office On Women's Health.*

32 Jasmine Wu, 2019, "Ugly Is In: How Crocs Have Taken Over Teen Footwear, And Sent The Stock Soaring," *CNBC.*

33 "4 Things Veterinarians, Pet Marketers Must Know About Gen Z, Millennials," 2018, *Veterinary Practice News.*

Kenneth Matos, the industrial and organizational psychologist whom I introduced earlier, shared an example of a colleague who helps students get internships and jobs. Millennial clients of hers were on board with traveling and working for no pay or no direct link to their long-term career goals. Basically, if the job was interesting, it didn't matter if it was something amazing to put on a resume, because it provided a good experience. Gen Zers are far different; we want our resumes to be polished and any potential job or internship to be relevant in securing our financial and career success. Even if a certain position may help us in an indirect way, we'd much rather go the safer route.

This is even more relevant in the case of unpaid internships. Paid college internships are a great way to avoid amassing crippling amounts of debt. Taking on unpaid work does nothing to mitigate this. There's also psychological benefits, as we have a greater sense of self-worth and attachment to a paid job.

When millennials entered the workforce and the economy was strong, there was a mentality where being fired or laid off wasn't an enormous deal, because there was enough of a job market that finding new work wouldn't be too tough. That proved to not be the case when the recession hit, but at least early on, a fear over being terminated was not very present on a generation-wide scale.

Now that Gen Z is starting to work, our main priority is keeping our main job, even if work-life balance suffers. Even if we have other ventures or side jobs providing supplemental income and backup plans, our main focus is keeping the primary job that we earned. If there's a boss or company culture that perpetuates a sense that underperformers will be cut, it can likely cause burnout or unnecessary stress. What if you're sick for a few weeks? What if your job gets outsourced? If there's a subliminal, ever-present threat of being laid off or fired, it becomes a significant detriment to our performance and contributes to the anxiety that already grips our generation.

The relationship between companies and employees is changing too. Years ago, if an employee stayed with a company for a sizable chunk of time, job security was high. Baby boomers and older Gen Xers could stay at the same company for pretty much their whole careers, comfortably climbing the corporate ladder.

This changed in recent years to a figurative employment contract. "Employees and employers used to get married," said Matos. "Now, they just date."

The accepted mentality was that, at many firms, companies had an upper hand and could basically say to employees, "You'll work here until we no longer need you." The thinking, made popular by former General Electric CEO John Welch, is that low-performing employees, say, the bottom 10 percent, should be cut annually, allowing room to hire fresh talent and create a high-achieving culture. It worked well for GE, and they experienced massive growth. But it's a very controversial tactic. It dehumanizes employees, turning them into mere assets for the C-suite to manipulate, and grants employers massive leverage over employees. Because employees are then stacked or ranked against each other, a company culture forms akin to paranoia. Few companies openly state anymore that they follow a similar model, but I'm sure we can all think of companies that are fond of kicking out employees.[34]

Employees feel betrayed in this model, especially if their appeals fall on deaf ears after being terminated. Millennials have been pushing for more transparent employee termination policies and abolishment of the annual performance review. I personally feel that this is one of millennials' biggest contributions to the way we do work: changing the dynamic between employers and employees and rehumanizing work.

According to Matos, baby boomers and Gen Xers (for the most part) accepted that employers typically have the upper hand. Millennials feel belittled, and they're fighting back to

34 Max Nisen, 2015, "How Millennials Forced GE To Scrap Performance Reviews," *The Atlantic*.

put employees and employers even ground. Gen Zers, however, are coming into the workplace fully expecting to be treated as equals. We're approaching work, whether at big corporations or budding startups, as a partnership. In exchange for doing good work, we expect to be compensated and treated fairly, otherwise we'll leave.

You can offer sparkling benefits or pay however much you want (within reason, of course. If you're paying huge bonuses, this argument falls apart), but if Gen Zers feel as if this unwritten agreement has swung out of balance, they'll leave. A toxic work environment can take on many forms, but a constant fear of being terminated, when coupled with our competitive nature, will cause an immense amount of stress until we decide to leave, burn out, or are terminated.

This all sounds great on paper. But change is hard. Imagine a C-suite executive who had to go through the culling of low-performing employees throughout her career and not only survived, but is at the top of the company. She may believe that it's only fair for new employees to go through the same process. Or perhaps that giving companies the upper hand through handpicking top performers and cutting the rest is the best way to go, especially since it got her where she is now. And since decisions and company culture tends to flow from upper management down, this much-needed change would never take place. It takes a company-wide push to grant this level of transparency and openness.

The future of work is uncertain. We aren't sure to what extent AI, climate change, outsourcing, and other factors will impact the way we do work. And if, for instance, AI ends up taking a bunch of jobs, new employees in more entry-level positions will likely be the most expendable. According to the Brookings Institute, a major American think tank, almost half of the current work (49 percent) now being done by workers aged sixteen to twenty-four could be automated through the adoption of current technologies.[35] For Gen Zers who are already worried that the work they do may become automated or otherwise replaced, establishing this sense of security is incredibly important.

Key Takeaways:

- We are practical and cautious: Risks are, well, risky. Our main goal is to secure our personal bottom lines and make sure we have a steady financial future. We seek good compensation, sound benefits, and the opportunity to progress within a company.
- Create a safe working environment: Not in terms of preventing accidents (though that should be a priority,

---

35 Mark Muro, Robert Maxim, and Jacob Whiton, 2019, "Automation And Artificial Intelligence: How Machines Are Affecting People And Places," *Brookings Institute.*

anyway), but in terms of job security. In the long-term, productivity will suffer with the fear of termination. When recruiting or trying to retain employees, a solid strategy is to emphasize that employees stick around for a while and progress within the company. If this isn't really the case at your company, capitalize on company-wide initiatives to retain and reward hardworking employees.

- There's a shift in the balance: Younger employees want to be toe-to-toe with employers, and Gen Z has come to expect this equality. Gen Zers don't view themselves as mere assets for a company to constantly reevaluate and potentially discard. If a sense of candor and transparency between company executives and new hires is established, especially when it comes to long-term goals for the company, turnover will plummet and Gen Zers will be excited for the future growth of the company. It's the difference between working a dreary nine to five, where a single hiccup or misstep could get you fired, and being genuinely enthusiastic about where you work, having an openness to explore and innovate.

WHO WE ARE AND
WHAT WE BELIEVE

———

When I was pitching the idea of this book to a friend, he jokingly suggested, "You should call it 'Tired and Stressed-Out.'" And honestly, it's true. People thought millennials were anxious, but Gen Z is taking it to a whole other level.

Just look at the awful race for college admissions. High schoolers spend every waking hour maintaining perfect GPAs, bouncing between extracurriculars, and poring over SAT practice books. Naively, I thought that once I entered college, students would be less stressed out. However, it seems that once the hurdle of getting into college was crossed, many immediately began to focus on their next long-term goal. Students who are competing with each other for top slots, such as pre-med and pre-law students, seem to be especially burned out.

At my large, competitive public high school, many students had perfect 4.0 GPAs and a laundry list of extracurricular activities. Everyone copes with stress differently, and it was clear that some top performers were beginning to burn out well before entering college. It wasn't just limited to the straight-A students; most students were very focused on, and worried about, getting into selective schools. For many, the goal was to get into UNC-Chapel Hill or NC State, two excellent local public schools. I remember the days that early application decisions came out for these schools. The atmosphere of the school felt "defeated" in a way—even the students who made it into these schools seemed deflated, having worked so hard to get there. And students that didn't get in felt devastated and worthless, even though college admissions are just a crapshoot with more luck involved than anything.

"I tutor and coach students who are in high school and applying to college," said Sravya Kuchibotla, a freshman at Harvard University who went to my high school. "When asking students what school they want to attend, I've literally gotten responses like 'the most competitive one' and 'the one with the lowest acceptance rate,' even if that school may not be the best in terms of the environment or the majors that are available."

Overall, school kickstarts a level of competition between peers that, in my opinion, is fiercer than most competition in the job-seeking world. At Duke University, which prides itself on being a rigorous school with a "work hard, play hard" mentality (I hate that phrase), many students pull all-nighters leading up to finals. It's all in the hopes of bumping that B+ to an A-, which will give a marginal boost to their GPA, which will make recruiters more interested, which will grant that JP Morgan internship, which will . . . and you see where this incredibly stressful line of thinking goes.

This same knowledge that everyone is in the same boat, however, can lead to ignorance. "There's a stress culture," said Sravya. "It's almost a greeting, right? We're like, 'How are you?' and they say, 'Oh, my God, I'm so tired. I got up so early.' Instead of asking why that's so or offering help, we say, 'Oh, yeah, me too.' We connect over the fact that we're tired and stressed."

Seventy percent of teens report that anxiety and depression is a "major problem" among their peers, and an additional 26 percent say it's a minor problem.[36] For comparison, less than three-in-ten teens say they feel a lot of pressure to look

---

36 Juliana Horowitz and Nikki Graf, 2019, "Most U.S. Teens See Anxiety, Depression As Major Problems," *Pew Research Center.*

good, and even fewer report feeling a lot of pressure to fit in socially.[37]

Poor mental health is definitely a major issue among our generation. Dr. Cindy Liu, a psychologist at Brigham and Women's Hospital, led a 2018 survey of over 67,000 college students to assess mental health. One in five students directly stated that they had thought of suicide. Alarmingly, one in ten said that they had attempted it. Both statistics are twice the national average for adults.[38]

There are many other significant stressors in our life. Recent mass shootings, especially in schools, have caused a considerable amount of anxiety. Three-in-four Gen Zers say mass shootings are a significant cause of stress. It's incredibly disheartening—now, when we go to school, we aren't just worried about grades and fitting in, but about whether we'll be safe.[39] Current efforts to prevent shootings, such as installing metal detectors or arming teachers, come with their own range of problems. There's a sense of hopelessness attached to this issue—despite national walkouts, protests, and marches, our efforts feel inconsequential toward curbing the risk of another shooting.

---

37 Ibid.
38 Italo Brown, 2018, "3 Out Of 4 College Students Say They're Stressed, Many Report Suicidal Thoughts," *ABC News*.
39 "STRESS IN AMERICA™ GENERATION Z," 2019, *American Psychological Association*.

And as mentioned in earlier chapters, there's a lot of political stress worldwide. Today, half of Republicans say they hate Democrats and almost half of Democrats say they hate Republicans. Lots of hate in general. Fifty-five percent of Gen Zers say the current political climate is a source of stress in their lives, and over two-thirds feel stressed about America's future in general.[40]

But at least at schools, there's a support network for people who are stressed out or depressed. Most school systems and colleges recognize the growing pandemic of poor mental health and have resources in place to help students. Beyond more formal measures, however, there's also a tiny bit of reassurance that it's not just you who's struggling. I haven't done this experiment myself, but based off one-on-one conversations, I'd estimate that the majority of freshman students enrolled in Econ 101, a large, difficult class at Duke, would raise their hands if I asked who felt overwhelmed. I watched my close friends pull all-nighters and struggle on homework assignments, and so, in an odd way, it's comforting to know that we're all struggling together.

But what happens when Gen Z enters the workforce? These support systems suddenly disappear. Instead of that warm and cozy feeling of knowing we're all suffering together, we're

---

40 Ibid.

pressured not to appear weak. Though some companies do it better than others, most lack the same kind of support systems for employees' mental well-being that colleges do. When considering that we spend half our waking hours at work (and oftentimes more) during adulthood, it's evident that our mental health will impact, and be impacted by, our work.[41] Unfortunately, there's a strong stigma against having poor mental health and a bias against those who appear to be depressed, overly anxious, or otherwise have mental afflictions.

Kenneth Matos states why this is an issue. "As the workforce becomes more diverse, not just in race, ethnicity, or gender, but also in things like mental and physical health and abilities, organizations are going to realize that the talents they want don't always come in the same package. They need to provide support for the full range of human experience if they're really going to get the best and the brightest for all their positions."

Adding to the problem is that employees themselves want to mask any mental afflictions, as they believe showing them is a sign of weakness. The line of thinking is "Who would want to promote a (depressed, anxious, etc.) employee if there are others who appear to be mentally stronger?" The truth is that

---

41 Karl Thompson, 2019, "What Percentage Of Your Life Will You Spend At Work?," *Revisesociology*.

there is a huge stigma against people with mental issues, and because of this, many try to hide their afflictions and do not seek treatment or help, making these problems worse.

"There are measurable losses associated with disclosing a mental illness," wrote Dr. Indigo Triplett, founder of Indigo Insights, a nonprofit that provides mental health assistance. "It's common for the mentally ill to be taken off a project that is perceivably high profile or stressful. Then there is the real chance of losing a job. Of course, we hear that people are protected under the Americans with Disabilities Act (ADA); employers must accommodate the mentally ill just as they do the physically ill. But that often does not happen. People are sometimes shamed or harassed into quitting."[42]

"It's fascinating to me that people would rather their coworkers think that they're at home with diarrhea than they're at home recuperating from, you know, lack of sleep, or stress, or grief, or any of these things that do contribute to our overall mental health," said Gabe Howard on his podcast, The Psych Central Podcast.[43] He's a renowned speaker, author, and podcast host who lives with bipolar disorder himself.

---

42 Indigo Triplett, 2015, "The Real Reasons Employees Hide Mental Illness," *Inc.*.
43 "Psych Central Podcast - Gabe Howard," 2019, *Gabe Howard.*

Ninety-one percent of Gen Zers said they have experienced at least one physical or emotional symptom because of stress.[44] We're well on the way to being renamed the Burnout Generation. So, what can be done? Gen Zers are super stressed out, but many cope by putting even more work on their shoulders. We believe that if we achieve our goals, the added stress will have been worthwhile. It is pivotal that companies encourage employees to take time out for themselves. Killer fifty-plus hour workweeks, intense travel schedules, and strict deadlines typical of corporate lifestyles all fuel stress, and just like with previous generations, Gen Z will welcome this workaholic culture. "Yeah, I don't mind working Saturday," says a Gen Z employee as she cancels a weekend trip to the beach. "London? Sure," says another chronically sleep-deprived employee.

"At the same time, the high percentage of Gen Z reporting fair or poor mental health could be an indicator that they are more aware of and accepting of mental health issues," said the American Psychological Association's chief executive officer Arthur C. Evans Jr., PhD. "Their openness to mental health topics represents an opportunity to start discussions about managing their stress, no matter the cause."[45]

44 "STRESS IN AMERICA™ GENERATION Z," *American Psychological Association.*

45 Sophie Bethune, 2019, "Gen Z More Likely To Report Mental Health Concerns," *American Psychological Association.*

Many of us will work our butts off, avoiding breaks and chances to hit reset. If employers reinforce breakneck work habits, the stress culture that has been hounding us since our school years will continue to be at the forefront, causing (at the very least) burnout. But, as Dr. Evans mentioned, this generation is also very receptive of the stressors in our lives and therefore open to help on handling stress.

Some companies do this very well. Business consulting firm EY has a program called "r u ok?" As the name of the program suggests, it's built upon asking coworkers if they're truly doing alright, dismantling the stigma surrounding mental health and providing resources such as cross-country presentations, virtual events, and follow-up services. "We need to have the right culture—one where people trust that coming forward about their struggle with mental health will not affect their job," says Dr. Sandra Turner, leader of the program. She said that within the first three months of the program's implementation, the EY Assist line pertaining to mental health received a 30.2 percent increase in calls.[46] In the typically stressful world of consulting, this was a much-needed program.

But while these programs are nice, ultimately, it's up to an employee's coworkers and manager to lead change. This is a

---

46 Tori Utley, 2017, "How EY Is Tackling Stigma And Promoting Mental Health For Employees."

delicate area, due to how easy it is to inappropriately infringe upon an employee's personal life and details. Gabe Howard said, "If you have a coworker who obviously is sick, you can go up and say, 'Are you okay? You don't sound real good.' But what do you do when you think they might be having an episode of depression? This is where it gets really, really tricky."[47]

I'm not a psychiatrist, or a psychologist, or a brain person at all, and so I'm not well-qualified to give medical advice. Overall, however, little steps in the right direction can help. The key is to foster a culture of understanding. By shoving aside pre-existing biases surrounding mental issues and giving mental health the same level of importance as physical health, the workplace will feel a lot more inclusive and accommodating. Your company can have an award-winning program for addressing employee mental health, but unless you allow candid conversations to flow regarding mental health, the stigma will not be broken. To sum it up, if a boss fosters the idea that, "Hey, if you're feeling stressed out, talk to me about it and I'll see how I can help," employees will feel much more comfortable.

There is a ton of advice online about how managers can help employees with mental health and well-being as a whole.

---

47 "Psych Central Podcast - Gabe Howard," *Gabe Howard.*

They all revolve around the same key concepts: listen attentively, encourage a healthy lifestyle in and out of the office, and adopt a constructive mentality (interestingly, however, no one mentions actually giving less stressful work to employees).

One key thing, however, is that this prioritizing of employee mental health needs to be proactive and at the forefront. First impressions count, and companies that emphasize their commitment to employee well-being from the get-go create a more welcoming environment for new hires.

How? As usual, it boils down to a shift in company culture. "Supervisors and leaders of the organization should be equipped to recommend resources to get employees the help they need," said American Heart Association CEO Nancy Brown in an interview with Human Resource Executive.[48]

"But the most important thing HR can do is to make sure that all employees understand the resources that are embedded in the company's offerings, such as through the health-insurance plan or the employee-assistance program. For so many people who don't normally think about accessing those benefits, they just don't know where to start. And think about how those features are highlighted; there are ways HR leaders

---

48 Jen Colletta, 2019, "7 Ways To (Effectively) Address Mental Health In The Workplace," *Human Resource Executive.*

can make sure they're promoted, and in a way that reduces stigma and encourages participation."

This emphasis on a company's offerings is especially relevant in training. Mentioning your company's robust mental health support system early on during training and explaining how to find company resources is far more important than the ping pong table or Friday evening Nerf gun fights. Even if the new hire doesn't have anxiety or any other mental affliction, it paints a picture of how supportive your company can be at the very least. This is the key to everything I've been pulling together so far: Gen Zers want their employers to be supportive and have employees' well-being in mind.

Let's delve into all the different things that stress out Gen Z (there's a lot). Of course, on an individual level, everyone has their own experiences and stressors in life. But there are many generational factors that contribute to our poor mental health.

So far, I've mentioned academics and mass shootings, and touched on political dividedness. Ever since we were young, social issues have been plastered all over the news, shaping our lives and our opinions on the world and affecting us personally.

We grew up being taught that everyone is equal and that America is a land of equal opportunity. Yet, it's clear to see that inequality, especially in America, is pretty darn sharp.

For instance, take a look at race relations in America. An NBC poll held in 2018 reveals that over 64 percent of Americans think racism is a major problem in our society.[49] There's been a number of high-profile cases where minorities were discriminated against. Incidents such as arrests made at Starbucks, a student napping in a Yale common room, and violence against minorities are all over the media, and Gen Zers are among the most outspoken against them. Even at Duke, a premier educational institute where students should be able to learn without fear, there have been a number of hateful incidents, such as swastikas being painted and etched all over campus.

Inequality, in everything from sexual orientation to income, has become center stage in large part due to social media's enormous influence (though it always has been a large issue). As an example, the Black Lives Matter movement sprung up in 2013 after the acquittal of George Zimmerman, who shot and killed African American teen Trayvon Martin the year prior. It's picked up a tremendous amount of steam on social

49 Andrew Arenge, Stephanie Perry, and Dartunorro Clark, 2018, "Poll: 64 Percent Of Americans Say Racism Remains A Major Problem," *NBC News*.

media. And it's not a single, isolated incident that caused this. Instead of just facing microaggressions and small-scale forms of racism, blacks and other minority groups feel fearful for their lives.[50]

A lot of this newfound hate comes in relation to Donald Trump's recent election and the resurgence of the alt-right. The majority of Americans think racism has gotten worse under the current administration. According to Pew, 65 percent of people believe it has become more common for people to express racist or racially insensitive views under the new administration.[51]

Gen Zers are the most racially and ethnically diverse generation ever. Almost half—about 48 percent—of Gen Zers in America are non-white, as opposed to 39 percent of millennials and 30 percent of Gen Xers.[52]

Because we're such a diverse generation, these racially-charged incidents tend to affect many of us personally. For instance, in February 2019, US Immigration and Cus-

50 "Herstory - Black Lives Matter," 2019, *Black Lives Matter*.

51 Juliana Horowitz, Anna Brown, and Kiana Cox, 2019, "Views On Race In America 2019," *Pew Research Center's Social & Demographic Trends Project*.

52 Richard Fry and Kim Parker, 2018, "'Post-Millennial' Generation On Track To Be Most Diverse, Best-Educated," *Pew Research Center's Social & Demographic Trends Project*.

toms Enforcement (ICE) led raids all across North Carolina, arresting around 200 individuals. There was a lot of backlash, and many students at Duke campus felt extremely fearful during this time, afraid to venture beyond campus.

Gen Z's diversity stretches beyond race. Less than two-thirds of Gen Zers identify as "exclusively heterosexual." For reference, 71 percent of millennials, 85 percent of Gen Xers, and 88 percent of baby boomers say the same. In the US, about seven in ten of Generation Z and millennials (72 percent and 69 percent respectively) have no problem with homosexual relationships. Only 43 percent of baby boomers feel the same way. [53] This impacts us on multiple levels; not only are we more tolerant of others' beliefs and expression-of-self, but we recognize that this diversity is a great thing, enabling a level of thoughtful discussion far greater than anything an otherwise homogeneous group of people would be able to produce.

Gender stereotypes are breaking down as well. Traditional, sometimes sexist beliefs are being tossed out the window. As we begin to enter the workforce, dismantling these stereotypes is paramount. Many companies have been making efforts to be more accepting of women, but it's going to reach

53 "BEYOND BINARY - The Lives And Choices Of Generation Z," 2018, *Ipsos MORI.*

a whole other level once Gen Z enters the workforce and pushes even more strongly for these changes.

As another example, look at computer science education in America. For as long as the discipline has been around, computer science has been an exclusively male-dominated field. Women weren't encouraged to tinker with computers and felt out of place in computer science classes. However, there are now many nonprofits, scholarships, and college-led initiatives designed to break down gender barriers in computer science, such as Girls Who Code, a very successful nonprofit supporting women in computer science. A lot of students at Duke are women in tech, and it's awesome to see this systematic breakdown of gender stereotypes at the educational level.

Expanding upon this is the feminist movement. It's bloomed into an international movement, where women of all nationalities feel inspired to break these gender stereotypes. Online campaigns, such as #MeToo and #everydaysexism, are fueled by our generation's desire to bring equality for all. Our generation is full of inspirational women leading social change, such as Malala Yousafzai, a Pakistani advocate for women's education and the youngest ever Nobel Prize laureate, and Emma González, survivor of the Stoneman Douglas High School shooting and advocate for gun control.

To be clear, our generation's progressiveness doesn't necessarily mark a distinct change in political views. Research on our political views is still very young and few concrete conclusions can be made until a significant chunk of Gen Z starts voting in elections. It's more that progressive individuals have found the support and networks to let their thoughts be heard.

Overall, Gen Zers are more likely to be accepting of who we are as individuals and place less judgement on others for being different. We've cultivated an atmosphere of acceptance. Social media has provided us with a platform to let our voices be heard in celebrating diversity, despite many thinking that it would do the opposite, propagating widespread cyberbullying. To be clear, there are a lot of crappy people on the internet, and they have the power to really hurt people, but for the most part, the block button has become a powerful tool.

Twitter in particular is a favorite among us due to how easily social issues can go viral—content is easily re-sharable by millions of users, allowing our posts to be amplified beyond one's immediate followers. In a nutshell, we've come to expect a more accepting culture, where once-marginalized groups are being helped the same as others and brought to their fullest potential. We want to break down social issues that plagued the generations before us to truly make a more inclusive and equal society.

I mentioned how companies are making strides to give women the same opportunities and equality in the workplace, but quite frankly, Gen Z won't see it as enough. In an era where it's commonly believed that someone's race, gender, sexuality, background, and more shouldn't affect their ability to succeed in the working world, we want true equality.

Promoting diversity and inclusion must be a priority for companies. Whether you're at a budding startup or a well-known corporation, a commitment to employees of all backgrounds is a must. This all sounds like common sense, but these efforts are oftentimes low-priority for companies with dozens of other budgets to juggle. Sixty-three percent of Gen Zers feel it is important to work with people with diverse education and skill levels. On top of that, an additional 20 percent think that having people of different cultures (ethnicity or origins) is the most important element to a team.[54] And since 77 percent of Gen Z says that a company's level of diversity impacts their decision to work there,[55] having a diverse workplace is pivotal for attracting and retaining employees of the new generation.

A big roadblock is the juxtaposition of wanting top-tier talent and wanting to hire from underrepresented backgrounds. I

---

54 "Failure Drives Innovation, According To EY Survey On Gen Z," 2018, *PR Newswire*.
55 Ryan Jenkins, 2019, "Statistics Exposing What Generation Z Wants From The Workplace," *blog.Ryan-Jenkins.com*.

talked with Paul Campbell, PhD, for more insight. He's the co-founder of the Brown Venture Group, which focuses on investing capital in early-stage tech startups run by people of color. "My passion, long-term, is to help others understand where the root causes of issues [surrounding diversity] are, so we can begin to actually make solutions versus just grasping at straws and not understanding where we can begin to solve these problems."

People from backgrounds with less opportunity may not have the same depth of experience as "more qualified" candidates, but still be very capable workers. This isn't something new to Gen Z, but becomes very relevant now as employers hire experienced workers while still claiming to want to hire folks from diverse backgrounds, even when these people may not have the same opportunities.

"What you find is, [especially] in Silicon Valley, many who are starting these companies up were able to start coding at thirteen or fourteen because they had access to Internet and other opportunities that diverse communities don't have," said Campbell.

And so, companies fall back to what they're comfortable with. If someone comes from a well-connected background or went to a top school, employers and recruiters are naturally drawn to them since there's almost an assumption that if someone has this attractive background, they'll be an ideal employee. "What happens is this halo effect: naturally, people gravitate toward things they're familiar with . . . because it's something you can anchor onto," said Campbell.

If you work a software firm and you see someone with years of coding experience, a sexy GitHub page, hackathon awards, etc., it's tough to potentially look at another candidate with limited accolades on paper, even if you're aware that he or she may not have had a privileged background. I keep using tech as an example, but this becomes even more relevant in very structured industries, such as just about anything in finance, where candidates succeed if they have completed rigorous(-ish) coursework in college, gotten a good SAT score, have connections in high places, and more.

Something pivotal here, however, is how often diversity programs fail. Companies have been using the same tactics since the 1960s, failing to address the institutional issues that further hinder diversity efforts. Companies try to fight biases with supposedly objective hiring tests for applicants. Many investment banks and consulting firms ask applicants to solve math and scenario-based problems on the spot. For instance, Kellogg professor Lauren Rivera observed hiring meetings at one firm.[56] The team barely paid attention when

---

56 Lauren Rivera, 2016, *Pedigree: How Elite Students Get Elite Jobs*, Princeton: Princeton University Press.

white men failed the math test but paid much closer attention when women and blacks did. Whether this was deliberate or not is beyond the point—an effort to reduce bias actually amplified it.[57]

As a note, this doesn't apply to each and every candidate. I'm using the term "diverse background" to highlight people who haven't had some of the same opportunities that many "ideal candidates" to top firms might, due to factors ranging from socioeconomic status to school systems to just about anything.

So what's the solution? Companies need to step up even before the hiring process. "Companies need to invest with local community, nonprofits, organizations to [create] a pipeline, to create experience by giving opportunities," said Campbell. When it comes time for internships and full-time roles, these programs can show companies that talented individuals may not have had the same four-year degree background as competitors, but they excelled at the opportunities they had.

It's tough for companies, since this means investing more money into providing these opportunities and training new hires, but it has a range of positive consequences. Not only will there be a breadth of experience and backgrounds rep-

---

57 Frank Dobbin and Alexandra Kalev, 2016, "Why Diversity Programs Fail," *Harvard Business Review.*

resented in new hires that lead to diversity in thought and expression, but employees will feel much more connected to their employer, reducing turnover that has come to be expected with younger workers. Intuitively, if a potential employee feels like local company A has been doing a lot to help them succeed on a personal level, like funding local education initiatives, he or she will feel a stronger connection to the company.

Ultimately, it boils down to care. If a big tech company full of white dudes hires a worker from a minority background, chances are he or she feels at least somewhat out-of-place unless it's evident that the company is making an effort to continue hiring people from diverse backgrounds. Gen Zers will feel much more at home if a company shows that it shares the same core values as Gen Zers, such as a commitment to diversity (along with a dedication to the environment and a desire to promote social equality through efforts within the company and with the greater community). Truthfully, having empty promises and multimillion-dollar diversity initiatives tend to do very little and is the easy way out. Instead, a cultural shift within the company must take place to ensure that Gen Zers are treated equally and feel welcome.

Key Takeaways:
- The Burnout Generation?: We're anxious and have poor mental health when compared to previous generations.

It's not just traditional academic stress and societal is-sues—we even fear shootings at our schools. Companies must encourage employees to take time for themselves, or else we will quickly become the Burnout Generation: the most promising generation that fizzled out way too soon.

- Socially Aware: Social media and the overall growth of the internet has allowed for activism and social issues to take the stage. We are very outspoken about social issues we feel strongly about and expect companies to do the same. Environmental, social, and diversity initiatives, to name a few, will strengthen Gen Zers' desire to work at a company and likely result in higher Gen Z employee retention.

- Diversity: Between race, sexuality, views, beliefs, and more, we're the most diverse generation ever. Companies must make a true commitment to improving diversity dynamics within the company if they want Gen Zers to be excited about working there. We recognize that this diversity in background makes for stronger teams and a stronger company, and we expect that companies recognize and celebrate the same thing.

MEANINGFUL WORK

——

"I don't want your hope," said Greta Thunberg. "I want you to panic. I want you to feel the fear I do. Every day. And want you to act. I want you to behave like our house is on fire. Because it is."

Thunberg has taken the world by storm. She's a Swedish environmental activist who has become the face of a global movement to raise awareness for climate change, leading school walk-outs to protest a lack of action toward curbing climate change.

"For way too long, the politicians and the people in power have gotten away with not doing anything at all to fight the climate crisis and the ecological crisis," she told the crowd at an Extinction Rebellion rally in the UK. "But we will make sure that they will not get away with it any longer."[58]

She's inspired millions of students and raised an unprecedented amount of awareness over this issue. Oh, and she's sixteen years old.

On September 20, 2019, climate change protests took place in over 150 countries with over four million participants, according to 350.org, a major environmental advocacy group that co-organized the strikes.[59] The vast majority of protesters were young people—students skipping class and lecture to fight for what they're passionate about.

It shouldn't come as a surprise, then, that this generation is the most purpose-driven generation yet. In a Canadian study of over 2,000 people aged between fourteen and thirty-six years old, they found that Gen Zers were far more purpose-driven and interested in meaningful work than millennials. "While millennials seek jobs that provide stability, convenience, and balance, Generation Z is more readily concerned with fueling their passions and taking pride

---

58 "German Students Walk Out Of School In Climate Change Protest," 2019, *Reuters*.
59 Jenny Tuazon, 2019, "Over 4 Million Join The Global Climate Strike," *350.Org*.

in the work they do. For the first time, we see a generation prioritizing purpose in their work."[60]

That's not to say that millennials aren't purpose-driven. But Gen Zers across surveys and studies consistently rank purpose and meaning in work far higher than older generations do.

In the case of climate change, our generation is very concerned and eager to spark change. It's something we find incredibly meaningful, in large part because, well, we fear the extinction of humanity. Not exactly something fun to look forward to. But even if climate change continues its course and humanity isn't wiped out, we know that quality of life worldwide will be severely diminished. When we strike or protest, for whatever cause we believe in, it fills us with purpose. We're each making an impact, however small, that can shape the world for the better.

This is all great on a grander, more global scale, but we bring about a sense of purpose in smaller, more personal ways too.

Cooking in college is tough. The motivation isn't really there, considering the dozens of dining options within easy walking distance. During finals week, I ordered an astonishing

---

60 "The Change Generation Report - Lovell Corporation," 2017, *Lovell Corporation*.

amount of takeout under the excuse that I was too busy studying (in reality, I was binging *Game of Thrones*). College is a neat little bubble where food is always on hand.

But cooking remains a popular activity among students during the school year. Though I consider myself a mediocre cook, from time to time (aka very rarely) I like to go beyond simply microwaving last night's leftovers and try my luck with a pot and stove.

Nothing I cook is restaurant quality. For instance, when I asked my friends to rate my pasta, they used really encouraging terms like "bland" and "undercooked." I'd like to think I'm improving, but that might just be wishful thinking.

From a rational perspective, cooking doesn't seem to be the best option. It eats up valuable time that could be spent doing homework or, better yet, sleeping. It also takes far more effort than simply walking to the nearest restaurant. Though ingredients may be healthier, every poorly made meal I make has a risk of salmonella. And it is only slightly cheaper, since I tend to get ingredients from pricier grocery stores near campus.

Based off just these reasons, it's clear to see that the cons outweigh the pros. But these were all measurable metrics:

nutrition, cost, effort. What about the immeasurable things? The happiness derived from cooking?

Personally, I like cooking because every time I cook, I learn something new and useful. But above all else, I feel an immense amount of pride and accomplishment after making a dish.

Simply put, I find meaning in cooking.

"Meaningfulness is really the experience that something is positive, purposeful, and significant . . . Purpose almost asks the question, 'What use are you to the world and to other people?' Do the things that bring you joy match up with utility to other human beings?" said Zach Mercurio, PhD, bestselling author and keynote speaker on purposeful leadership and meaningful work.

Over nine out of ten American workers spanning all generations are willing to trade a percentage of lifetime earnings for greater meaning at work. "On average, employees will give up 23 percent of their total future lifetime earnings—nearly a quarter of their income—in exchange for work that is always meaningful."[61]

61   Shawn Anchor, Andrew Reece, Gabriella Kellerman, and Alexi Robichaux, 2018, "9 Out Of 10 People Are Willing To Earn Less Money To Do More-Meaningful Work," *Harvard Business Review*.

And so, meaningful work isn't something new to Gen Z. But it's a huge priority for Gen Zers, who would happily leave a job that lacks meaning.

As I talked with Zach, it became clear that meaningful work differs from person to person. "You can do what you love to do [and follow] your passions . . . but unless they have a broader impact, then they're relatively self-serving and self-limiting in terms of fulfilment," he said.

For one employee, purposeful work might mean whatever contributes the most to the company's bottom line; for another, it could be work that allows him to create new, cutting edge-technology. However, as Zach said, work has to tie in with a broader impact.

Simply having a job or role that seems to be meaningful doesn't necessarily make it so. "I know plenty of people that work in social impact enterprises that find their work purposeless and meaningless," he said. Essentially they, along with people in other fields you think would lead meaningful careers, don't have a clear view of how the work they're doing directly affects people.

And so a key way to make work meaningful is to show how the work that someone is doing directly impacts others' lives. We need to prioritize increasing visibility between an employee and the people who are affected at the end. If you work at a financial services company, for instance, it can be easy to lose track of the bigger picture when crunching numbers. But by seeing how your work impacts people putting their life savings in the company and praying for a happy retirement, work becomes much more meaningful. Gen Z employees will quickly lose heart unless they see the broader impact of the work they do.

"Can you tell me one product on planet Earth that does not have a human being at the end of its supply or service chain?," asked Mercurio. "Every job exists to solve a human problem, or fill a human need, or the company wouldn't exist. One of the keys in the future for cultivating [meaningful] workplaces for Gen Z is to make sure that they directly understand the human being that's at the end of the equation."

Mercurio brought up a famous story from the Cold War. American President John F. Kennedy toured the NASA facility in 1961. He interrupted the tour to talk to a janitor carrying a broom. "Hi, I'm Jack Kennedy. What are you doing?"

"Well, Mr. President," the janitor said, "I'm helping put a man on the moon."

The janitor saw the bigger picture. Sure, he wasn't the one being strapped into the rocket, but he knew how his work, which many would ignore or loathe doing, impacted the success of the mission.

We, as a generation, have grown up trying to define what is meaningful to us. While millennials grew up hearing things like "follow your dreams," we Gen Zers grew up with a much more pragmatic, cautious mentality. We've been taught to follow and stay true to our core values, and in doing so already have an inkling of what we find meaningful in work, even if we haven't entered the job market yet. I think there's an obviously simple solution to granting a meaningful work environment: ask what the employee finds purposeful and foster that sense of purpose.

So while asking may seem like an overly simple solution, it works. Asking something along the lines of "What are the problems you want to solve that are impacting people, and how do your unique strengths tie into this?" There are overall trends, of course: Gen Zers value social impact, being given responsibility, etc. But Gen Z is the most diverse generation yet in terms of experiences and backgrounds. The only way to home in on what any one Gen Z employee wants in the workplace is to ask. (Note: Try to foster a truly honest conversation when this happens. If a boss asks out of the blue, "What do you find meaningful?" it comes across as an interview-esque question, and the employee might say something wishy-washy in an attempt to shy away from answering the question. Stress that you want to make work as meaningful as possible. Foster a genuine conversation.)

To be clear, this search for meaning extends beyond the occasional cooked meal. At Duke, students are involved in everything from hip hop dance to journalism, a cappella to club figure skating. And for many, these aren't just fun after-class activities, but hobbies and interests they want to tie in with their career aspirations. Our generation has adopted a unique mindset: instead of separating our fun hobbies from a nine to five job we may otherwise dislike, we want to tie these interests into our careers. Examples are all over campus: pre-med students who want to figure out how music and medicine tie together, or computer science whizzes who want to use their love of basketball to make sports data analytics more robust.

We aren't sure whether or not Gen Z will follow in millennials' footsteps and change jobs relatively frequently early in careers, simply because Gen Z has to be in the workforce for a couple years to know so. But as we've explored, Gen Z is really interested in job stability.

This is a long-winded way of saying that Gen Z may not have the same level of "job hopping" characteristics as millennials have, instead trying to tie in their personal interests and talents with their work rather than immediately jumping ship.

Research here is not solid, and it'll take time to truly figure out, but this is where Gen Z seems to be headed. This could mean requesting a project that interests them or finding creative and interesting ways to benefit the company. And so, it is more important than ever for companies to cultivate meaningful work and have a purpose worth committing to, because if Gen Zers can't build up this sense of meaning in the work they do, they'll be incredibly demotivated.

What this means is that Gen Z employees need the freedom to explore. This is easier to do at smaller companies, since new employees oftentimes don multiple hats and gain a breadth of exposure to different parts of the company. But at bigger companies, especially those with more a more stratified and rigid hierarchy, employees oftentimes get pigeonholed in work they don't want to do.

There's a lot of ways to grant new employees this flexibility, which we'll explore further in the last chapter. Rotational programs are amazing at giving new employees this exposure to different jobs and roles, helping them explore where their interests may be. For companies with the means to offer these extensive programs, it's an amazing solution. But there are other, less expensive methods, too. A lot of this ability to explore and come up with solutions boils down to leadership.

The pros and cons of different leadership styles have been shared for decades. If you lead a team, however large, you have likely heard of terms like "laissez-faire" and "autocratic," fancy terms to sum up whether someone prefers to assign work and then nap, or breathe down employees' necks, and everything else in-between. Given Gen Z's desire for independence and responsibility with the work they do, there should be a push toward less autocratic leadership of new employees.

This goes against a lot of common business philosophy. The accepted idea is that if employees lack much experience or knowledge, such as Gen Zers who just entered the workforce, management should be more autocratic and micromanaging.[62] This belief has served well in the past, but it's sure to spark friction as this new generation enters the workforce. As mentioned, Gen Zers are very independent and take initiative to figure things out on their own. There's a strong do-it-yourself mentality. And Gen Z has mastered the Internet, so there's less of a reliance on bosses for help when the answer could be a few keystrokes or taps away. All of this makes for a new type of worker, one that needs more autonomy to perform meaningful and productive work.

---

62 "6 Ways Autocratic Leadership Can Actually Work," 2018, *Mindvalley Blog.*

"This generation prefers that their managers act more like coaches instead of bosses," says Laura Weldy, ICF-credentialed life coach at The Well Supported Woman. "For this to be effective, managers should understand the difference between coaching, which involves powerful, thought-provoking questions to unlock potential and inspire self-realization, and micromanaging, where a leader provides all the answers and acts more like a taskmaster."[63]

That doesn't mean employees should be left out to dry. Training is more paramount than ever, and Gen Z employees want to make sure they have the resources available to deliver top-notch work. But at the same time, micromanaging can do more harm than good. Companies need to avoid doling out cookie-cutter work and create an environment where employees can take chances with their work without fear of failure.

As an ending note, I'd like to focus on what employees can do for themselves to foster meaningfulness as well. "You have way more control over how you feel about your work than we exercise, all of us," said Mercurio. This sense of purpose is very critical and has huge repercussions on success—he states that people who are purpose-oriented are 50 percent more likely to be promoted. Beyond this, everyone wants to have a

63   Kiely Kuligowski, 2019, "What Businesses Should Know About Working With Gen Z," *Diversityinhighereducation.com.*

fulfilling career. Crafting a personal mission statement helps drive this sense of purpose. Instead of just thinking about the next task completed or the next career move, having a contribution mentality by thinking about how the work you do impacts people down the pipeline is pivotal for success and fulfillment.

To sum up this section, here are three big tips to guide managers of the innovation generation:

- Go the laissez-faire route: Or at the very least, don't try to micromanage everything your peers or employees are doing. It's not so much about having projects with open-ended interpretations—imagine how disastrous that could be when building, say, a prosthetic robotic arm—but giving workers the autonomy to tackle projects with their own unique methodology and thought processes.
- Just ask: Meaningful work is hard to define for everybody. We all differ as people, and what one person might find meaningful may not mean anything to another person. Gen Zers already know, to some degree, what kind of work they want to do in life, and so simply asking employees what they find meaningful can help tremendously in both how you manage Gen Z workers and how to cultivate meaningful work.

- Foster meaningful work: Gen Zers aren't motivated as much by cash or fancy titles as older generations. Overall, they seek responsibility, freedom to pursue interests in the workplace, and the potential for hard work to turn into career advancement. Find out what motivates each of your workers and try your best to align company goals with that search for meaning.
- But take it a step further. Gen Zers might have a sense of what they find meaningful, but haven't fully developed this idea yet since they're just entering the workforce. Allow workers to explore different aspects of their career and experiment with other roles and responsibilities within a company.

THOUGHTFUL GAMIFICATION OF THE WORKPLACE

—

Whether attempting a tricky penalty kick, repairing a tank, or mining for diamonds, many Gen Zers love to immerse themselves in the world of video games. Gaming has always been a popular hobby, but the industry has experienced monumental growth over the past few years. In the US, the video game industry had a revenue of approximately $43.4 billion in 2018, an 18 percent improvement over 2017.[64] And

---

64 "2019 Essential Facts About The Computer And Video Game Industry - Entertainment Software Association," 2019, *Entertainment Software Association.*

now, it's the most popular form of entertainment in the world.[65]

Many factors can be attributed to the rapid growth of the gaming industry, such as easy accessibility due to mobile devices, better graphics, a robust multiplayer community, and the popularity of streaming gaming sessions on services like YouTube and Twitch.[66] The video game industry has done a fantastic job of creating products and services for new generations.

Personally, video games are far more fun with friends, especially when playing with others in the same room instead of online. Mario Kart Wii is a favorite of mine, a very popular game where you can race against your friends using Mario franchise characters. There's nothing more satisfying than going from dead last to first, all the while joking with my friends. This highlights an important aspect of video games that is oftentimes overlooked: they typically involve other people. Whether competing or collaborating, we love using immersive experiences as a means of socializing with others.

A big question that we've been answering, piece-by-piece, is how to give Gen Zers meaningful and engaging work. We

---

65 "Investing In The Soaring Popularity Of Gaming," 2018, *Reuters*.
66 *Entertainment Software Association.*

know how important this sense of engagement is for Gen Zers, and if they aren't motivated by their work, they'll leave. Training is a huge component to this engagement, and taking a look at video games, and games as a whole, can offer a potential solution.

Gamification is a buzzword right now, and for good reason. If applied correctly, it can create new opportunities for growth in a company. And Gen Z loves it. In a study conducted by Kahoot!, a popular game-based learning platform, 48 percent of Gen Zers surveyed say they prefer to learn through gamification or game-based learning methods.[67] Given that this report is from a gamification platform, I took it with a grain of salt. However, the methodology of conducting the survey was sound, save for the fact that participants had been exposed to the concept of gamification before. Still, it's a fairly significant proportion, and other studies corroborate that Gen Z is far more enthusiastic about it than other generations.

That doesn't mean turning an office into an arcade. But the principles behind video games can be applied, especially relevant now that Gen Z is entering the workforce. Gamifying the workplace is crucial for the future.

---

67 "Press Release: Kahoot! Edtrends Report 2018 For Corporate Trainers," 2018, *Kahoot!*.

I talked to Yu-kai Chou, an early pioneer of gamification, for more insight. He's the author of *Actionable Gamification* and a founding partner at the Octalysis Group, a consulting group that focuses on gamification.

"There's a trend in terms of why the world needs gamification, and why it's becoming more and more relevant," Chou said. As a society, "we're focusing more attention on how the brain works and how to engage the brain. Commercially, companies are using this to get people to be more addicted, but internally, companies are trying to get employees to be more inspired or more motivated to work."

Gamification is especially relevant in fields that may be considered *cough* boring. Slower-moving industries like finance, healthcare, and law could greatly boost employee engagement through the use of gamification techniques. But since these are typically hierarchical industries that aim to exude professionalism, upper management may be less willing to try something like gamification. On the other end, says Chou, is education, which has welcomed gamification with open arms. Unfortunately, school systems and other companies in the education field typically lack the immense amount of funding other industries have and cannot make significant forays into new concepts such as gamification.

This discrepancy between eager industries with little funding and unenthusiastic businesses with overflowing pockets highlights why despite all the hype and fanfare over gamification, businesses have been slow to adopt gamification methods. Another factor, Chou says, has to do with the fact that companies who tried to implement gamification techniques in the past had lackluster results. In late 2012, research and advisory company Gartner predicted that by 2014, 80 percent of then-current gamification applications would fail to meet business objectives "primarily due to poor design," a statistic which turned out to be quite accurate.[68] Since then, despite years of trial-and-error, most companies *still* fail to capitalize on an immense opportunity, and their efforts fall flat.

Gamification is tricky to get right, but the purpose of this chapter is not simply to discuss the pros and cons of gamification techniques (a Google search brings up thousands of articles toting the benefits and pitfalls of gamification). It's to reveal how to leverage these techniques specifically for Gen Z in the most impactful way.

To be clear, despite the name, gamification is not just about making work a game. I drew parallels with video games to simply highlight Gen Z's familiarity with the concept of gamification. It is about using psychological techniques to mo-

---

68 Ivan Kuo, 2013, "80% Of Bad Gamification Initiatives Still On Track To Fail By 2014," *Gamification Co.*

tivate workers, thereby boosting productivity and business. According to Gabe Zichermann, author of *Gamification by Design*, "gamification is 75 percent psychology and 25 percent technology."[69]

Applying gamification methods doesn't require a radical dismantling of the current corporate system. Companies, at least theoretically, already reward strong performers with higher compensation and advancement opportunities. But Gen Zers don't value fancy titles as much as older generations, particularly Gen Xers and baby boomers.[70] Engaging Gen Z through gamification requires gaming elements tailored toward this generation's needs and wants.

Here's an example: for a club project in high school, two friends and I coded a video game that taught financial principles for college. We knew that learning personal finance was not a particularly engaging activity for most students, nor was it something emphasized in our school system. So, we made a simple, text-based game where the player starts off their college journey, juggling credit costs, tuition, food plan purchases, and more while trying to maintain a budget. The aim of the game was simple: don't be in debt and have

69 Gabe Zichermann and Christopher Cunningham, 2011, *Gamification By Design: Implementing Game Mechanics In Web And Mobile Apps*, Sebastopol, CA: O'Reilly Media.
70 Jackie Wiles, 2019, "The Real Impact On Employees Of Removing Performance Ratings," *Gartner*.

more money than any other player. Whichever player ended with the highest remaining budget would win a $15 gift card.

The game audience was limited to students of our large public high school, but it became popular. This was in large part due to our own marketing efforts within the school, but we were still surprised when the play count surpassed 1,000. When asking students why they continued to play over and over again, we received a few common responses:

- Accessible game design: The game was accessed through a link and could be played on any browser—it even saved progress. The game was in black-and-white without fancy graphics or other clutter (mostly because our coding skills weren't very good), and this made it very appealing. Bored at lunch? Sitting on the bus? Load up the game.
- Intrinsic motivation: At first, we thought students were playing the game repeatedly to try to win the gift card, but many weren't even aware there was a prize. Many players felt that they were genuinely learning useful concepts. This motivation, when combined with wanting to beat previous high scores, led some to play dozens of times.
- Fun: We knew that convincing people to play a basic text-based game was a hard sell, so we tried to make it as fun and engaging as possible. Scenarios players encountered in the game were funny (though I might be a bit biased

in saying so), and far from the typical "personal finance is boring" idea.

Now, I'm not going to pretend that this was some huge research study. There were all sorts of other variables that could have influenced the game, and these responses were very informal. However, trends were still very apparent, and we were able to create something that a lot of students were able to enjoy.

This was a way of gamifying an otherwise complex and not incredibly interesting topic. In a nutshell, we were lucky and fairly successful, but most gamification applications aren't.

Many unsuccessful methods of gamification involve throwing shiny badges or other forms of "achievements" at employees. Chou points to the over-justification effect, where giving a reward for a task reduces intrinsic motivation for doing that task. Things like badges and points are extrinsic motivators, and once all the novelty and initial curiosity about a gamified system wears off, employees might feel even less motivated than before.

Brian Burke, research vice president of Gartner, agrees with this sentiment:

"The focus is on the obvious game mechanics, such as points, badges, and leaderboards, rather than the more subtle and more important game design elements, such as balancing competition and collaboration, or defining a meaningful game economy. As a result, in many cases, organizations are simply counting points, slapping meaningless badges on activities, and creating gamified applications that are simply not engaging for the target audience."[71]

But many programs that employ gamification overly pull on employees' competitive sides. "Usually, people don't like to be in a constant state of competition," says Chou. While very competitive gamification systems can make employees more driven and obsessive in the short run, over time, it can cause burnout.

As commonly performed in sales, brazenly displaying each employee's monthly or quarterly sales is a very crude yet effective competition-oriented method of gamifying employee work. Sales competitions can boost sales a good amount without completely burning out employees, but salespeople already have to worry about hitting targets—adding competition from within a company could be over-the-top and cause employees to overexert themselves. Despite the high employee turnover rate in sales (about 34.7 percent for busi-

---

71 "Newsroom," 2012, *Gartner.*

ness-to-business salespeople in the US in 2017)[72] businesses like sales competitions because of the added revenue. Typically, very competitive performers rise to the top of these competitions, but they are also more susceptible to burning out.

So currently, sales competitions have pros and cons that very roughly balance out. But what happens when it's not just a few salespeople that are fiercely competitive, but a sizable number of employees? Gen Z is the most competitive generation yet, and so a team of Gen Z employees fighting for top rankings would have very pronounced and noticeable effects.

Right now, Gen Zers are competing for top spots in scholarship programs, colleges, and internships. If you know any Gen Zers, the struggle to outperform peers is very taxing. All of that competition is driven by self-pressure to be the best, but imagine *encouraging* an even higher level of competition in the workplace. It would be mentally exhausting for employees and potentially create a toxic working environment. In addition, if there's an implicit threat that underperformers in any gamification situation could be let go, Gen Zers would be even more anxious and worried, especially since they value job security so much.

---

72 Anthony Chaine, 2017, "Why Is Turnover So High In B2B Sales?," *LinkedIn.*

With that being said, all over the internet, gamification coaches are offering advice on how to apply gamification methods successfully, but few account for the demographic change in the workforce soon to take place and the level of competitiveness that we Gen Zers have. If you read up on suggested ways to implement gamification in your workplace, shying away from purely competitive elements may be a good idea, especially if you are planning to hire fresh graduates soon.

Now the complete absence of competition would not be ideal either; competition is a strong motivator, especially for Gen Z. So how do you strike this balance? I talked to Chou at length to try to determine the most feasible solutions.

A solid idea is to implement small team competition. Essentially, instead of pitting individual employees against each other to rack up sales, learn a technology the quickest, etc., splitting employees into small groups to go head-to-head against each other works very well. There's obviously still a competitive element, but the urgency and anxiety of individual employees is diminished. No one wants to let their team down, but the entire experience is a lot friendlier and more collaborative.

Let's look at the sales competition example again. If there are twenty salespeople, splitting them into four or five teams could work very well. Ideally, each group would have a mix of top-performing, experienced salespeople, good performers, and recent hires.

Gamification, when applied successfully, works. Customer-facing applications work very well and are light-years ahead of what businesses are doing internally. Examples are everywhere: eBay's bidding system, "spin the wheel for a coupon" tactics, and the Nike Run Club, which uses personalized training and encouragement from friends on the app.

Cultivating a culture of healthy competition, where employees feel like they're actively learning and building a sense of personal growth, is crucial for this upcoming generation. Training methodology and recruitment needs to be overhauled, something we'll look at in the next chapter, and gamification of repetitive and less engaging aspects of work can make a huge impact.

Key Takeaways:
- Gamification is familiar: Gen Z has grown up experiencing examples of gamification all our lives. Gamified programs in a company will be relatively easier for Gen Zers to pick up and adopt.
- Gamification is tricky to get right: Especially for a generation used to well-designed games and gamification methods, lackluster implementations of gamification

in the workplace can appear, well, lackluster, and even counterproductive. The most ideal cases of gamification-based training builds around creating a sense of friendly competition where the stakes aren't super high (aka, avoiding offering big bonuses or threatening termination).

- Gamification fosters collaboration: Gamification typically implies competition, yet it can greatly boost a sense of connection between employees. If on day one, we get slammed with training documents and boring videos, it doesn't ease this transition. Gamification, especially when employed in small teams rather than individually, can contribute to strong team dynamics early on.

MENTORSHIP AND FEEDBACK

———

When Gen Z enters the workplace, Gen Xers and millennials will be moving up the rungs of management, and many new employees with little experience will find themselves in supervisory roles.

New workers are being given more and more responsibility, yet have no clue how to perform well. Especially as Gen Zers begin to favor smaller companies, they could have a huge amount of responsibilities with no one to turn to.

Let's focus on startups for a bit. It's well-known that most startups fail without guidance and mentorship because, especially if this is the founder's first try at a company, there's a whole lot to learn (many will still fail anyway). Mentors don't need to be world-famous executives, just people with a decent understanding of the entrepreneurial landscape.

Just take a look at Shark Tank, ABC's hit TV show (or Dragon's Den, the British equivalent). In it, entrepreneurs pitch their new startups to a panel of experienced—and rich—entrepreneurs and venture capitalists. If the judges, called sharks, are interested enough, they offer seed money in exchange for equity in the company. Between the high stakes and Kevin O'Leary's sparkling personality, the show has really pumped up enthusiasm for entrepreneurship.

Viewers oftentimes focus purely on the financials. How much is the startup worth? How much do the judges offer, and for what stake? But something that's largely overlooked are the judges themselves. They aren't just banks, but hugely successful people with a wealth of experience. Companies that are scooped up by a shark, or even multiple sharks, suddenly have guidance from some incredibly savvy and successful business owners.

Mentorship doesn't even have to be in-person, such as in the case of TED Talks. Certain Talks resonate with us, whether we watch it live or online. For the dozen or so minutes that a speaker is on stage, talking about anything from meditation to beatboxing, we're transfixed. We forget that the speaker is talking to dozens of people, millions if you count video viewers, and feel as if we're having a one-on-one meeting, learning something useful. In the age of the TED Talk, online videos and educational tools have become comparable to online mentors, even if we never communicate back with them. We're constantly motivated to improve ourselves, and mentors help us accomplish this.

This is all probably common sense—obviously mentors help us grow. But for younger generations, mentors are a need.

Millennials advocated for mentorship within a company, but many leave before a strong relationship is cemented. Millennials who plan on staying with their organization for over five years are twice as likely to have a mentor (68 percent) than not (32 percent).[73]

But for Gen Z, having that mentorship in the first place is a key deciding factor over whether to stay or not. In a survey of 5,000 Gen Zers, 33 percent said they believe a mentorship program is the most important workplace benefit, only a few percentage points behind health care benefits, the number one need.[74]

---

73 "The 2016 Deloitte Millennial Survey," 2016, *Deloitte*.
74 "What 5,000 Gen Z'ers Tell Us About The Future Of Work," 2017, *Medium*.

Mentors are incredibly useful, and we realize it. A family friend, coach, teacher, celebrity, or just about anyone can fulfill that role. They are especially important at companies. In the weeks after being hired, when everything at the company is new and shiny, company mentors show us the ropes. They are a wealth of knowledge, highlighting their career paths and mistakes they made along the way. And they aid tremendously in internal networking, helping us gain our footing and introduce ourselves to other employees who in turn can also offer input and advice. They kickstart a journey at any company, making the transition less jarring, and root for us to do our best.

Gen Zers don't want bosses—we want coaches. People who we are eager to work with every day and who prioritize the growth of their employees. And it's not just about having a single mentor, either. Social media sites, especially LinkedIn, have made it really easy to reach out to like-minded people. Entrepreneurs typically like to have a handful of mentors, each skilled in their own area.

And ultimately, people want to be mentors. It boils down to what we covered in the purpose section. Mentorship has a direct impact, where the effort you put in clearly affects another person's success. It's extremely fulfilling, a kind of volunteering for others' careers.

Many companies institute mentorship programs, with varying levels of success. Sodexo, a French food services and facilities management company, offers three different mentorship programs for employees at different stages of their careers. Peer-to-peer mentoring is very encouraged at any stage of the employee's career, but their mentorship programs aren't just for new employees. As the Sodexo website writes: "The IMPACT program has become a catalyst for many management careers throughout Sodexo. It is a structured, yearlong program designed for mid-level managers and above who are paired with executive-level mentors. The entire cohort comes together four times over the course of a year—once in person and three times via webinars—and each pairing meets individually throughout the same time period."[75]

As Sodexo shows, mentorship isn't just limited to young workers. To expand on this, something interesting is a concept called reverse mentoring. It's exactly what it sounds like. New, younger employees mentor more senior leaders at the company. It seems counterintuitive, but the topics these young mentors focus on aren't navigating office politics or meeting cool people within the company. Typically, they talk about newer technological trends that are rapidly changing the world.

75 Trish Freshwater, 2016, "Mentoring Makes An IMPACT On Employee Careers," *Sodexo*.

This unique form of mentorship comes with clear benefits on both ends. The mentor, a younger worker, is contributing to the company at the very top rungs of management and feels much more invested. Plus, since talking to senior management (let alone teaching them) can be nerve-wracking, it's an awesome opportunity for practicing effective communication. And then obviously, senior management has a better reading on trends shaping the world and learns more about key insights that could be used to keep a competitive edge.

"That is actually more beneficial than your traditional mentor-mentee relationship," said Ashira Prossack, multi-generational research expert, "because it really empowers the younger employee—it gives them confidence." And, she explained, it's an excellent way to break down generational barriers to create a more integrative environment.

Mentorship is changing, and it's a good thing. Mentors don't necessarily have to be older than the employee; if they have a different skill set and background, they can offer their own advice. Even if you are a young worker yourself and feel as if you don't have much to contribute, mentorship is a two-way street; new employees might learn a lot more than you think while offering actionable advice for your own careers.

Micro-mentorship will thrive. Gen Zers are go-getters and ambitious, and they will actively seek out mentorship where they can get it. A friend of mine made an Excel sheet listing people he met at his last internship who he considered to be mentors. Name, position, key things he learned, and even how likely he was to contact them five years down the line were a metric for how valuable that connection was. Truthfully, I found it a bit odd, especially the whole "likeliness to reach out to them in five years" part, but hey, it works for him. His goal? Hold on to the Excel sheet forever, tacking on extra tabs for the rest of his career as he stockpiles key mentors to guide him.

It's a touch over-the-top in my opinion—after all, we have LinkedIn—but it goes to show how much we want guidance. Honestly, work is scary, and it's a big reason why people decide to stick around for graduate school after completing an undergrad program (especially if the job market is poor). Mentors help ease that transition, and we're all for it.

Many times, a manager can fulfill a mentor role as well, but it's tricky. Gen Z is eager to learn, and without offering guidance and professional development, employees will leave, regardless of the other perks. A manager's main objective is to manage, achieving set goals and dealing with paperwork and other office interference that could slow down employees. And frankly, the same level of candor can't be achieved between an employee and boss. I don't think that an employee's boss would be super comfortable, for instance, if the employee was asking for help securing a promotion or a job outside the company. It's not impossible, though. If a boss wants to be a mentor to his or her employee, clear boundaries need to be set in advance, and most help would likely be through internal networking and professional development opportunities.

Gen Zers want mentorship, and a company doesn't need to have formal programs to facilitate this (though it would certainly help, since we'll be searching for these programs when applying to jobs). Mentoring an employee helps them get their bearings sooner and has been proven to lead to greater career success and engagement with the company.[76]

This increased communication isn't limited to mentor and mentee. As mentioned, a higher proportion of Gen Zers prefer face-to-face communication in the workplace than millennials, a trend that at first glance appears counterintuitive to our experience with technology. But on top of that, Gen Z expects continuous communication and feedback in the work we do.

A national study of over 1,000 Gen Zers and 1,000 millennials found that more than two-thirds of Gen Zers say they need feedback from their supervisor at least every few weeks,

---

76 Lauren Bidwell, 2019, "Why Mentors Matter: A Summary Of 30 Years Of Research," *SAP SuccessFactors.*

otherwise they'd quit. This compares to less than half of millennials. Furthermore, one in five Gen Zers said they need feedback daily or several times each day to stay with an employer.[77] I found this pretty astonishing.

"Feedback should not be confined just to the mentor," said Prossack. "Feedback needs to happen on the fly, continuously."

For many companies, formal performance reviews are the answer, but these aren't very effective. "The annual or twice-a-year performance review never worked for anyone," said Prossack. "It doesn't help an employee develop. Meeting with someone every six months does nothing."

Companies introduced these reviews in the '60s and '70s to provide a standardized grading system for managing larger companies more efficiently. It's an outdated form of review that gives little help or guidance to employees.[78] It typically does not measure an employees' passion, instead focusing on his/her deliverables, and most reviews are based off a manager's potentially spotty memory, which can lead to bias and poor feedback.

---

77   "Generation Z Research – State Of Gen Z™ 2018," *The Center For Generational Kinetics.*

78   Yuki Noguchi, 2014, "Behold The Entrenched — And Reviled — Annual Review," *NPR.*

Research firm CEB, a subsidiary of Gartner, found that 95 percent of managers are dissatisfied with the way their companies conduct performance reviews. In addition, they said that almost 90 percent of HR leaders say the process doesn't yield accurate information.[79] Through combing through many surveys, it appears that between 60 and 95 percent of employees are dissatisfied with these reviews.

For years now, people have been claiming that performance reviews are dead, but companies still use them—almost 90 percent, according to a 2014 survey.[80] It's an easy way to give *some* feedback, however ineffective, which is better than nothing. CEB published that, "Performance drops when ratings are removed. When Gartner originally studied the dynamic in 2016, performance dropped by around 10 percent. In 2018, that decline shrank to a still-significant 4 percent."[81]

"Employee performance tends to drop when ratings disappear because managers struggle to make and communicate performance and pay decisions without ratings," says Jeanine Prime, VP and Team Manager at Gartner, in the study.

---

79 Lillian Cunningham, 2015, "In Big Move, Accenture Will Get Rid Of Annual Performance Reviews And Rankings," *The Washington Post*.

80 "HR Professionals' Perceptions About Performance Management Effectiveness," 2014, *SHRM*.

81 Jackie Wiles, 2019, "The Real Impact On Employees Of Removing Performance Ratings," *Gartner*.

The problem arises when companies completely abolish performance reviews without taking any strong effort to lead more meaningful conversations and give feedback. Basically, instead of replacing reviews with other feedback systems, managers simply got rid of the only feedback mechanism they had.

To be clear, it's a two-way street. Court Lorenzini, the entrepreneur and mentor who I introduced earlier, highlights that it's tough for large organizations to rethink feedback and introduce a structural change. "For large scale deployment, what I think it comes down to is having informal [conversations] . . . there needs to be a willingness of the young person who's new to the job to seek their manager out face-to-face and say, 'How did I do?'"

Employees today are dissatisfied with how feedback is given, and Gen Zers, who care more about regular, meaningful feedback, will be even more dissatisfied as we settle into the workplace. Actions such as getting rid of performance reviews might seem to be a powerful statement that can spark a lot of change, but only if there is a proper feedback infrastructure to replace it.

Feedback and mentorship is a must. Managers need to make an effort to frequently check-in with employees, because a traditional annual performance review, when mixed with a few conversations throughout the year, do little to guide new workers. Even as our workweeks become busier and busier, carving out time to hold meaningful conversations with young workers needs to be a priority.

Key Takeaways:

- We love mentorship: We'll actively seek it too. It's one of Gen Z's top priorities and has become easier and more informal with the rise of technology and our willingness to branch out to others. Colleges teach us that our classmates and friends are greater resources than anything else the school has to offer, and that kind of mentality translates directly to the workplace.

- Mentorship is changing: Formal company mentorship programs are awesome, but not the only way to foster mentorship. The popularity of reverse mentorship, group mentoring sessions, and even career influencers on sites like LinkedIn mean that the once-narrow definition of one-on-one, senior to junior-level employee mentorship has changed.

- Feedback is a must: As a generation, we've grown up being given constant feedback and expect the same moving forward. In school, grades and comments helped us improve our abilities and succeed academically. In a rapidly-changing workplace, feedback is crucial for helping guide us to success.

THE WORKPLACE
OF THE FUTURE

———

"AI is a fundamental risk to the existence of human civilization," said Elon Musk, outspoken CEO of Tesla and SpaceX.[82] He, along with other tech leaders, have made it clear that unless we prepare proactively, artificial intelligence will destroy the world.

But on the flip side, many believe AI will have a very positive impact. Facebook CEO Mark Zuckerberg views AI optimistically, oftentimes butting heads with naysayers.[83]

———

82   Catherine Clifford, 2017, "Facebook CEO Mark Zuckerberg: Elon Musk's Doomsday AI Predictions Are 'Pretty Irresponsible,'" *CNBC*.
83   Ibid.

I think a quote sums up the issue. "By far, the greatest danger of Artificial Intelligence is that people conclude too early that they understand it," wrote Eliezer Yudkowsky, an AI researcher best known for coining the concept of "Friendly AI" in a 2002 paper.[84] Since then, AI has come a long way, but it still rings true.

People draw up predictions of how AI will evolve over time, but there are just too many variables at play to accurately project how it will impact us ten, fifteen, twenty years down the line.

We oftentimes look to high-profile tech leaders to explain the upsides and pitfalls of AI, but just about everyone has an opinion nowadays, ranging from "AI will create a new utopia" to "I have a bunker in the countryside for when the robots take over." Most people are somewhere in the middle in their opinions.

According to a study of over 2,000 consumers in the US, Canada, the UK, China, and Brazil, more people see AI's impact on society as a positive rather than a negative (45 percent versus 7 percent respectively), yet more consumers said AI will cause more job loss (82 percent) than job creation

---

84 Eliezer Yudkowsky, 2001. *Creating Friendly AI 1.0: The Analysis and Design of Benevolent Goal Architectures*, The Singularity Institute, San Francisco, CA.

(18 percent).[85] Overall, people seem quite trusting of AI in their daily lives, despite apprehension over how it will impact the job market.

I've been focusing a lot on AI because it exemplifies our fears and hopes. So much of the future of work seems to be built around the impact AI will have. In a nutshell, the future is uncertain. We're experiencing technological growth faster than anything we've seen before, and if it continues to accelerate, there's really no way to tell what the world will be like.

It's not only AI that makes the future uncertain. I mentioned climate change earlier to introduce purpose and meaning. Climate change is an issue that Gen Zers (and millennials too), really take to heart, in large part because the looming impact of climate change will affect us in our lifetimes and is already doing so. We've reached a point where doomsday predictions may actually occur within the next few decades (or even years), leaving us with a feeling of, well, doom.

As I've mentioned in previous chapters, this generation is anxious about the future, in large part due to lack of certainty and preparedness. No one knows what will happen.

---

85 Leslie Gaines-Ross, 2016, "What Do People — Not Techies, Not Companies — Think About Artificial Intelligence?," *Harvard Business Review.*

Because of this, when it comes to work, Gen Zers want to have as much experience, knowledge, and education as possible in order to have greater security moving forward. Through pursuing higher education, we're increasing our odds of being financially secure in the long-run, a feeling that largely outweighs our fears over student debt.

When I first began my research, I found that a lot of supposed Gen Z experts touted that Gen Zers were no longer interested in college, in large part due to the student debt epidemic. In truth, Gen Z is the most educated generation yet. According to the Pew Research Center, 59 percent of eighteen- to twenty-year-old Gen Zers are enrolled in college, as opposed to 53 percent of college-age millennials back in 2000, and this percentage is expected to rise as younger Gen Zers reach adulthood.[86]

So, despite fears over amassing college debt and having seen the impact of debt on millennials, Gen Zers are still electing to go to college. Having a college education is one of the most surefire ways to be an attractive applicant in an increasingly competitive job market, especially since many jobs require this education in the first place. And something that's widely overlooked is how comfortable college and further education

86 Richard Fry and Kim Parker, 2018, "'Post-Millennial' Generation On Track To Be Most Diverse, Best-Educated," *Pew Research Center's Social & Demographic Trends Project.*

is. If we aren't 100 percent sure about what we want to do in the future, going to graduate school seems like a great option—we can explore our interests further, get a higher degree under our belt, and put off jumping into a potentially volatile job market.

On top of this, Gen Zers have a knack for finding resources to boost understanding. Need help on a subject in class? Hop on Khan Academy or watch a YouTube video. A do-it-yourself attitude toward learning is crucial for the future, but without employer help when we enter the workforce, it may not be enough given the increasingly rapid changes in the workplace.

According to the World Economic Forum, "By 2022, no less than 54 percent of all employees will require significant re- and upskilling."[87] Employers need to take an active stance in teaching employees new skills, and block off time for this professional education.

Having employees spend a portion of the work week, however small, on learning new skills is essential for the future. It's tricky, considering how much work needs to be done in a given week, but it becomes an investment, making for more skilled employees.

---

87   "The Future Of Jobs Report 2018," 2019, *World Economic Forum.*

Plus, it aids in retention. A massive 93 percent of employees would stay at a company longer if it actively invested in their careers, according to LinkedIn's 2018 Workforce Learning Report, a statistic that includes members of all working generations.[88]

The future of training could be very interesting. Richard Adler, distinguished fellow at the Institute for the Future, says, "AI, voice-response, telepresence, VR, and gamification techniques will come together to create powerful new learning environments capable of personalizing and accelerating learning across a broad range of fields."[89]

As a computer science student, this sounds really exciting. But for the time being, the way we train employees is a little less advanced, yet equally as important.

A lot of companies nowadays prioritize training for hard skills. "How can we implement this new programming language? Or that new project road mapping tool?" The problem is that training for hard skills is essentially useless, since newer, shinier, more efficient technologies are released so rapidly. Hard skills nowadays have a relatively

---

88 "LinkedIn's 2018 Workplace Learning Report," 2019, *LinkedIn Learning*.

89 Dan Anderson, 2017, "Elon & Pew Research Report On The Future Of Jobs And Jobs Training," *Elon University*.

short shelf life, and employees get so used to a particular technology or way of thinking that innovation halts and skill gaps emerge.

Many of the people I interviewed indicated that prioritizing soft skills is the key to the future, especially for Gen Z. "The role of the employer now is to provide foundational training," said Ashira Prossack. "How do you write a business email, or a business memo? How do you interact with customers?"

We know how to develop hard skills and have been doing so all our lives. There seems to be a societal pressure to learn hard skills—it's far easier to convey to employers that you're skilled in a handful of programming languages than saying you have strong email-writing skills. It's something employers reinforce too, in stating that applicants must be qualified in a bunch of hard skills without quantifying how good they need to be in softer skills.

If we ever need to learn something new, Google is our best friend. But soft skills are arguably much more important in today's rapidly-evolving workplace, and it needs to be a priority when training Gen Z.

This isn't a new concept. Soft skills, like communication and problem-solving, are always in demand and will be resistant to automation. The same LinkedIn report states that according to its participants, a mix of talent development professionals and employees, training for soft skills is the number one priority for the future.

There are many ways to implement this learning without dropping productivity. Lunch-and-learn events are awesome, because they allow younger employees to learn what more senior employees do, see the overarching goals and values of the company, develop these soft skills, and foster a sense of mentorship. Training needs to have a human factor and pull from concepts of mentorship, gamification, and feedback in order to be successful. And since new employees, regardless of generation, oftentimes refrain from speaking up or asking questions for fear of appearing unintelligent or inexperienced, it's really important to foster this training from the get-go.

But the future of work isn't just about training. Terms like work-life balance and flexibility have really been in the headlines, and Gen Z is all for it.

"I rarely have to stay after five," said a programmer, barely older than me, proudly wearing a shirt with his company's name plastered on the front. "Plus, on most days, I arrive after ten. I'm not a huge morning person, so it definitely helps."

Whenever I roam around career fairs, most representatives at company booths are one of three people: recruiters, recently-graduated alumni employees, and older alumni employees. When describing their work, they each tend to stress different things.

"Our interns receive a project from the start that directly ties in with the company's goals," says a recruiter. "The work they do has a big impact on the company."

"We've started a mentorship program for new hires, and I recently took in a new engineer under my guidance," says an older employee.

Both of these lines are awesome, because they highlight things our generation wants. But what I've really noticed is that young employees who've come to represent their companies, some recently graduated, tend to really emphasize work-life balance above all else.

Of course, employers only say this when they foster a good work-life balance. I've never talked to an investment banker who said the work-life balance is great. But when this balance is there, it's very attractive for young employees.

This balance is important for all workers, regardless of generation or background. However, especially in America, which seems to idolize obsessing over work and clocking in an unhealthy number of hours, people don't seem to care. Or at the very least, they don't prioritize having a healthy balance over, say, job growth or compensation. Best case, we spend our lives pouring in countless evenings and weekends. Worst case, we die early. (I'm being a bit dramatic, but still.)

Work-life balance isn't limited to just hours. It's about the mental toll that work takes. Even if you work shorter hours than the average worker, if your mind is always "on," even at home, it can take a huge toll. And, it's about flexibility; having the time and resources to regain energy, pursue passions, and otherwise achieve this balance.

It's tricky, of course. There's always one more task to do, one more project to complete, one more email to send. Companies need to be active proponents for achieving this balance, otherwise we risk burning out fast.

The idea of flexibility has shifted throughout the years. It's not just about working from home if a spouse isn't feeling well, or taking time off for maternity or paternity leave, but about personalization. For one employee, that could mean having a refreshing midday walk, for another, it could mean not working weeknights to perform standup at local bars. And really, the only way to achieve this personalization is to ask employees what they want.

Granted, flexibility is a luxury. It can be challenging for employers to grant this level of autonomy, especially in roles with frequent, strict deadlines. And many employers view flexibility critically, fearing employees will take advantage of flexible work.

But it's a two-way street. According to an Accenture study, "83 percent of new graduates are willing to relocate to another city or region for the right job offer," while another 60 percent consider it acceptable to work evenings or weekends.[90] We are willing to sacrifice some components of flexibility, but in return, we expect a more personalized form of flexibility that is cognizant of our individual needs.

But it becomes an amazing selling point to new talent. Employees nowadays expect some degree of flexibility in their daily jobs, and Gen Zers are entering the workplace with the expectation that we'll have it. "Gen Z is so socially aware and so progressive, they're asking for things that older generations have been scared to ask for," said Ana Recio, executive vice president of global recruiting at Salesforce.[91] We assume that having this level of autonomy is part of the employment package to begin with.

---

90 Payal Vasudeva and Diana Barea, 2019, "Gen Z Rising," *Accenture.*
91 Claire Miller and Sanam Yar, 2019, "Young People Are Going To Save Us All From Office Life," *The New York Times.*

Work is constantly evolving, and companies need to be as progressive as possible to stay ahead of the curve. Between seeking higher education, wanting flexibility to pursue side work and hobbies, and prioritizing learning and development at work, it's evident that Gen Zers want to be as prepared as possible for what the future holds. However, once we graduate and spend so much of our time working, it becomes difficult to find time to learn new things on our own. That's why it's up to companies to support us and make us bulletproof for whatever the future holds.

Key Takeaways:

- The future of work is uncertain: As I've repeated over and over, no one really has a solid prediction for where technology is going, or at the very least, an exact timeframe. We've all seen how quickly new technologies pop up in the workplace, and this is only going to become more frequent as time goes on. Gen Zers are going through school worried about which jobs and tasks are "future-proof" and which will be outsourced or automated.

- Training needs to be a priority: We expect continuous learning and development. A short training program as soon as we get hired is a solid start, but companies need to be invested in their employees' long-term growth. In turn, employees will feel more connected to companies that are truly committed to helping them learn and explore.

- Flexibility is a must: The nine to five model is starting to break down, an indicator of changing views on rigid, inflexible work. But flexibility is not just about work hours. Many Gen Zers are perfectly fine working 50-hour work weeks but seek flexibility in other ways. This could mean anything from working evenings instead of mornings or taking a longer lunch break to play pickup basketball. Managers should ask employees what kinds of flexibility they want in the workplace and do their best to accommodate this, even if it may seem to be a hassle in the short-term.

ENDING COMMENTS

———

Overall, companies need to become far more progressive in order to attract and retain Gen Z talent. We have high expectations when entering the workforce, and companies that fail to meet this demand will lose a major competitive edge in hiring top talent.

This book was meant to offer a look into some of the trends that define our generation. Again, these are rough trends built upon research that largely consists of polls. If 80 percent of Gen Zers say they want something, that's a pretty large statistic, but at the same time, that means 20 percent don't. The book was designed as a tool to better understand us, not to make hard and fast rules and guidelines.

Hopefully, you have a better sense of who we are and how to lead us to success in the workplace. Prestige and pay have dropped in importance (relative to other factors) for Gen Z employees, and so it now requires far more attention and effort to engage with young employees. Managers and HR professionals need to be proactive in creating a company we would love to be a part of.

Gen Z, the largest generation in the world, has begun to enter the workplace. We have the ambition, adaptability, and mindset needed to navigate a rapidly-changing world. Under the right guidance, and as part of a diverse, innovative, and growth-minded company culture, we will be able to leave an enormous impact through our work.

Whether you're a manager, HR professional, Gen Zer yourself, or virtually anyone else, you will be working professionally with this newest cohort of workers for the rest of your lives. How will you contribute to the Gen Z revolution?

APPENDIX

What Makes Generations Different?

"Baby Boom Generation." 2019. *U-S-History.com.* https://www.u-s-history.com/pages/h2061.html.

Chamberlin, Jaime. 2009. "Overgeneralizing The Generations." *https://www.apa.org.* https://www.apa.org/monitor/2009/06/workplaces.

Fry, Richard. 2019. "Baby Boomers Are Staying In The Labor Force At Rates Not Seen In Generations For People Their Age." *Pew Research Center.* https://www.pewresearch.org/fact-tank/2019/07/24/baby-boomers-us-labor-force/.

"Generations And Age." 2019. *Pew Research Center.* https://www.pewresearch.org/topics/generations-and-age/.

Kane, Sally. 2019. "Learn The Common Characteristics Of Generation X Professionals." *The Common Characteristics Of Generation X Professionals.* https://www.thebalancecareers.com/common-characteristics-of-generation-x-professionals-2164682.

"The Generations Defined." 2019. *Pew Research Center.* https://www.pewresearch.org/fact-tank/2019/01/17/where-millennials-end-and-generation-z-begins/ft_19-01-17_generations_2019/.

Entrepreneurship and Side Hustles

"35% Of The U.S. Workforce Is Now Freelancing—10 Million More Than 5 Years Ago." 2019. *Fast Company.* https://www.fastcompany.com/90411808/35-of-the-u-s-workforce-is-now-freelancing-10-million-more-than-5-years-ago.

Branson, Richard. 2019. "Richard Branson On Intrapreneurs." *msnbc.com.* http://www.nbcnews.com/id/41359235/ns/business-small_business/t/richard-branson-intrapreneurs/#.XYGFIShKhPY.

"Freelancing In America: 2019 Survey - Upwork." 2019. *upwork.com.* https://www.upwork.com/i/freelancing-in-america/2019/.

"Media Attention For Entrepreneurship." 2019. *The World Bank.* https://tcdata360.worldbank.org/indicators/aps.entrp.media?country=USA&indicator=3113&countries=BRA&viz=line_chart&years=2003,2015&compareBy=region.

"Peter Szabo." 2019. https://peterszabo.co/.

Schawbel, Dan. 2014. "The High School Careers Study." *millennialbranding.com.* http://millennialbranding.com/2014/high-school-careers-study/.

"The 9th Annual State Of Entrepreneurship Address." 2018. *Ewing Marion Kauffman Foundation.* https://www.kauffman.org/what-we-do/entrepreneurship/policy/state-of-entrepreneurship-2018.

Digital Natives

Jenkins, Ryan. 2019. "This Is How Generation Z Will Communicate At Work." *Inc..* https://www.inc.com/ryan-jenkins/72-percent-of-generation-z-want-this-communication-at-work.html.

Moskowitz-Sweet, Gloria, and Erica Pelavin. 2019. "Generation Z Is Far More Nuanced About Tech Than Its Predecessors." *Pacific Standard.* https://psmag.com/ideas/what-you-can-learn-from-your-gen-z-kid-about-technology.

"Realizing 2030: A Divided Vision Of The Future." 2019. *Dell Technologies.* https://www.delltechnologies.com/content/dam/delltechnologies/assets/perspectives/2030/pdf/Realizing-2030-A-Divided-Vision-of-the-Future-Summary.pdf.

Schawbel, Dan. 2019. "Gen Y And Gen Z Global Workplace Expectations Study." *millennialbranding.com.* http://millennialbranding.com/2014/geny-genz-global-workplace-expectations-study/.

"What Gen Z Thinks About Payments." 2019. https://seekingalpha.com/article/4261923-gen-z-thinks-payments.

Social Media in the Workplace

"#Brandsgetreal: Social Media & The Evolution Of Transparency." 2019. *Sprout Social.* https://sproutsocial.com/insights/data/social-media-transparency/.

"Annual Gen Z Research Studies – Trends, Stats, Attitudes & More." 2019. *The Center For Generational Kinetics.* https://genhq.com/annual-gen-z-research-study/.

King, Alan. 2017. *Brown Dog Photo.* Image. https://images. unsplash.com/photo-1505628346881-b72b27e84530?ixlib=rb-1.2.1&ixid=eyJhcHBfaWQiOjEyMDd9&auto=fo rmat&fit=crop&w=934&q=80.

Medina, John. 2019. "Vision | Brain Rules |." *brainrules.net.* http://www.brainrules.net/vision.

"The Social Economy: Unlocking Value And Productivity Through Social Technologies." 2012. *McKinsey & Company.* https://www.mckinsey.com/industries/high-tech/ our-insights/the-social-economy.

Young, Katie. 2018. "3 Ways Gen Z And Millennials Use Social Media Differently - Globalwebindex Blog." *Globalwebindex Blog.* https://blog.globalwebindex.com/trends/3-ways-gen-z-millennials-use-social-media-differently/.

Stability

"4 Things Veterinarians, Pet Marketers Must Know About Gen Z, Millennials." 2018. *Veterinary Practice News.*

https://www.veterinarypracticenews.com/4-things-vet-erinarians-pet-marketers-must-know-gen-z-millenni-als/.

Adamy, Janet. 2019. "Gen Z Is Coming To Your Office. Get Ready To Adapt.." *WSJ*. https://www.wsj.com/graphics/genz-is-coming-to-your-office/.

"Decrease In Teen Pregnancy." 2019. *Office On Women's Health.* https://www.womenshealth.gov/30-achievements/09.

"Deloitte Research Reveals A "Generation Disrupted": Growing Up In A World Of Accelerated Transformation Leaves Millennials And Gen Zs Feeling Unsettled About The Future." 2019. *Deloitte.* https://www2.deloitte.com/global/en/pages/about-deloitte/press-releases/deloitte-millennial-survey-research-reveals-gen-z-un-settled.html.

Hobbes, Michael. 2018. "Generation Screwed." *The Huffington Post.* https://highline.huffingtonpost.com/articles/en/poor-millennials/.

Muro, Mark, Robert Maxim, and Jacob Whiton. 2019. "Automation And Artificial Intelligence: How Machines Are Affecting People And Places." *Brookings Institute.* https://www.brookings.edu/research/automation-and-artificial-intelligence-how-machines-affect-people-and-places/.

Nisen, Max. 2015. "How Millennials Forced GE To Scrap Performance Reviews." *The Atlantic*. https://www.theatlantic.com/politics/archive/2015/08/how-millennials-forced-ge-to-scrap-performance-reviews/432585/.

Streaks, Jennifer. 2018. "Black Families Have 10 Times Less Wealth Than Whites And The Gap Is Widening—Here's Why." *CNBC*. https://www.cnbc.com/2018/05/18/credit-inequality-contributes-to-the-racial-wealth-gap.html.

Wu, Jasmine. 2019. "Ugly Is In: How Crocs Have Taken Over Teen Footwear, And Sent The Stock Soaring." *CNBC*. https://www.cnbc.com/2019/07/15/ugly-is-in-crocs-have-taken-over-teen-footwear-and-boosted-its-stock.html.

Who We Are and What We Believe

Arenge, Andrew, Stephanie Perry, and Dartunorro Clark. 2018. "Poll: 64 Percent Of Americans Say Racism Remains A Major Problem." *NBC News*. https://www.nbcnews.com/politics/politics-news/poll-64-percent-americans-say-racism-remains-major-problem-n877536.

Bethune, Sophie. 2019. "Gen Z More Likely To Report Mental Health Concerns." *American Psychological Association.* https://www.apa.org/monitor/2019/01/gen-z.

"BEYOND BINARY - The Lives And Choices Of Generation Z." 2018. *Ipsos MORI.* https://www.ipsos.com/sites/default/files/2018-08/ipsos_-_beyond_binary_-_the_lives_and_choices_of_gen_z.pdf.

Brown, Italo. 2018. "3 Out Of 4 College Students Say They're Stressed, Many Report Suicidal Thoughts." *ABC News.* https://abcnews.go.com/GMA/college-students-stressed-report-suicidal-thoughts-study/story?id=57646236.

Colletta, Jen. 2019. "7 Ways To (Effectively) Address Mental Health In The Workplace." *Human Resource Executive.* https://hrexecutive.com/7-ways-to-effectively-address-mental-health-in-the-workplace/.

Dobbin, Frank, and Alexandra Kalev. 2016. "Why Diversity Programs Fail." *Harvard Business Review.* https://hbr.org/2016/07/why-diversity-programs-fail.

"Failure Drives Innovation, According To EY Survey On Gen Z." 2018. *PR Newswire.* https://www.prnewswire.com/news-releases/failure-drives-innovation-according-to-ey-survey-on-gen-z-300714436.html.

Fry, Richard, and Kim Parker. 2018. "'Post-Millennial' Generation On Track To Be Most Diverse, Best-Educated." *Pew Research Center's Social & Demographic Trends Project.* https://www.pewsocialtrends.org/2018/11/15/early-benchmarks-show-post-millennials-on-track-to-be-most-diverse-best-educated-generation-yet/.

"Herstory - Black Lives Matter." 2019. *Black Lives Matter.* https://blacklivesmatter.com/herstory/.

Horowitz, Juliana, and Nikki Graf. 2019. "Most U.S. Teens See Anxiety, Depression As Major Problems." *Pew Research Center.* https://www.pewsocialtrends.org/2019/02/20/most-u-s-teens-see-anxiety-and-depression-as-a-major-problem-among-their-peers/.

Horowitz, Juliana, Anna Brown, and Kiana Cox. 2019. "Views On Race In America 2019." *Pew Research Center's Social & Demographic Trends Project.* https://www.pewsocialtrends.org/2019/04/09/race-in-america-2019/.

Jenkins, Ryan. 2019. "Statistics Exposing What Generation Z Wants From The Workplace." *blog.Ryan-Jenkins.com.*

https://blog.ryan-jenkins.com/statistics-exposing-what-generation-z-wants-from-the-workplace.

"Psych Central Podcast - Gabe Howard." 2019. *Gabe Howard.* http://www.gabehoward.com/psych-central-podcast/.

Rivera, Lauren. 2016. *Pedigree: How Elite Students Get Elite Jobs.* Princeton: Princeton University Press.

"STRESS IN AMERICA™ GENERATION Z." 2019. *American Psychological Association.* https://www.apa.org/news/press/releases/stress/2018/stress-gen-z.pdf.

Thompson, Karl. 2019. "What Percentage Of Your Life Will You Spend At Work?." *Revisesociology.* https://revisesociology.co m/20 16/08/16/percentage-life-work/.

Triplett, Indigo. 2015. "The Real Reasons Employees Hide Mental Illness." *Inc..* https://www.inc.com/indigo-triplett/the-real-reasons-employees-hide-mental-illness.html.

Utley, Tori. 2017. "How EY Is Tackling Stigma And Promoting Mental Health For Employees." https://www.forbes.com/sites/toriutley/2017/05/30/how-one-company-normalized-mental-health-and-encouraged-employees-to-ask-for-help/#73270bfc6dc9.

Meaningful Work

"6 Ways Autocratic Leadership Can Actually Work." 2018. *Mindvalley Blog.* https://blog.mindvalley.com/autocratic-leadership/.

Anchor, Shawn, Andrew Reece, Gabriella Kellerman, and Alexi Robichaux. 2018. "9 Out Of 10 People Are Willing To Earn Less Money To Do More-Meaningful Work." *Harvard Business Review.* https://hbr.org/2018/11/9-out-of-10-people-are-willing-to-earn-less-money-to-do-more-meaningful-work.

"German Students Walk Out Of School In Climate Change Protest." 2019. *Reuters.* https://af.reuters.com/article/worldNews/idAFKCN1QI4YP.

Kuligowski, Kiely. 2019. "What Businesses Should Know About Working With Gen Z | Diversity Jobs And Employment." *diversityinhighereducation.com.* https://diversityinhighereducation.com/news/What-Businesses-Should-Know-About-Working-With-Gen-Z.

"The Change Generation Report - Lovell Corporation." 2017. *Lovell Corporation.* https://www.lovellcorporation.com/the-change-generation-report/.

Tuazon, Jenny. 2019. "Over 4 Million Join The Global Climate Strike." *350.Org*. https://350.org/over-4-million-join-the-global-climate-strike/.

Gamification

"2019 Essential Facts About The Computer And Video Game Industry - Entertainment Software Association." 2019. *Entertainment Software Association*. https://www.theesa.com/esa-research/2019-essential-facts-about-the-computer-and-video-game-industry/.

Chaine, Anthony. 2017. "Why Is Turnover So High In B2B Sales?." *LinkedIn*. https://www.linkedin.com/pulse/why-turnover-so-high-b2b-sales-anthony-chaine/.

"Generation Z Research – State Of Gen Z™ 2018 – The Center For Generational Kinetics." 2019. *The Center For Generational Kinetics*. https://genhq.com/generation-z-research-2018/.

"Investing In The Soaring Popularity Of Gaming." 2018. *Reuters*. https://www.reuters.com/sponsored/article/popularity-of-gaming?.

Kuo, Ivan. 2013. "80% Of Bad Gamification Initiatives Still On Track To Fail By 2014." *Gamification Co.*

https://www.gamification.co/2013/12/18/gartner-bad-gamification-initiatives-still-fail-2014/.

"Newsroom." 2012. *Gartner*. http://www.gartner.com/newsroom/id/2251015.

"Press Release: Kahoot! Edtrends Report 2018 For Corporate Trainers." 2018. *Kahoot!*. https://kahoot.com/press/2018/12/04/training-gen-z-workplace-edtrends-report/.

Zichermann, Gabe, and Christopher Cunningham. 2011. *Gamification By Design: Implementing Game Mechanics In Web And Mobile Apps*. Sebastopol, CA: O'Reilly Media.

Mentorship and Feedback

Bidwell, Lauren. 2019. "Why Mentors Matter: A Summary Of 30 Years Of Research." *SAP SuccessFactors*. https://www.successfactors.com/resources/knowledge-hub/why-mentors-matter.html.

Cunningham, Lillian. 2015. "In Big Move, Accenture Will Get Rid Of Annual Performance Reviews And Rankings." *The Washington Post*. https://www.washingtonpost.com/news/on-leadership/wp/2015/07/21/

in-big-move-accenture-will-get-rid-of-annual-performance-reviews-and-rankings/.

Freshwater, Trish. 2016. "Mentoring Makes An IMPACT On Employee Careers." *Sodexo.* http://www.sodexo. jobs/career_connection/883286/article4.htm.

"HR Professionals' Perceptions About Performance Management Effectiveness." 2014. *SHRM.* https://www.shrm. org/hr-today/trends-and-forecasting/research-and-surveys/Pages/2014-performance-management.aspx.

Noguchi, Yuki. 2014. "Behold The Entrenched — And Reviled — Annual Review." *NPR.* https://www.npr.org/2014/10/28/358636126/ behold-the-entrenched-and-reviled-annual-review.

"The 2016 Deloitte Millennial Survey." 2016. *Deloitte.* https://www2.deloitte.com/content/dam/Deloitte/ global/Documents/About-Deloitte/gx-millenial-survey-2016-exec-summary.pdf.

"What 5,000 Gen Z'ers Tell Us About The Future Of Work." 2017. *Medium.* https://medium.com/@doorofclubs/ what-5-000-gen-zers-tell-us-about-the-future-of-work-6dd00f796e8f.

Wiles, Jackie. 2019. "The Real Impact On Employees Of Removing Performance Ratings." *Gartner*. https://www.gartner.com/smarterwithgartner/corporate-hr-removing-performance-ratings-is-unlikely-to-improve-performance/.

The Workplace of the Future

Anderson, Dan. 2017. "Elon & Pew Research Report On The Future Of Jobs And Jobs Training." *Elon University*. https://www.elon.edu/u/news/2017/05/02/elon-pew-research-report-on-the-future-of-jobs-and-jobs-training/.

Clifford, Catherine. 2017. "Facebook CEO Mark Zuckerberg: Elon Musk's Doomsday AI Predictions Are 'Pretty Irresponsible.'" *CNBC*. https://www.cnbc.com/2017/07/24/mark-zuckerberg-elon-musks-doomsday-ai-predictions-are-irresponsible.html.

Fry, Richard, and Kim Parker. 2018. "'Post-Millennial' Generation On Track To Be Most Diverse, Best-Educated." *Pew Research Center's Social & Demographic Trends Project*. https://www.pewsocialtrends.org/2018/11/15/early-benchmarks-show-post-millennials-on-track-to-be-most-diverse-best-educated-generation-yet/.

Gaines-Ross, Leslie. 2016. "What Do People — Not Techies, Not Companies — Think About Artificial Intelligence?." *Harvard Business Review.* https://hbr.org/2016/10/what-do-people-not-techies-not-companies-think-about-artificial-intelligence.

"LinkedIn's 2018 Workplace Learning Report." 2019. *LinkedIn Learning.* https://learning.linkedin.com/resources/workplace-learning-report-2018?trk=lilblog_02-27-18_WLR-2018-launch-blog_tl&cid=70132000001AyziAAC.

Miller, Claire, and Sanam Yar. 2019. "Young People Are Going To Save Us All From Office Life." *The New York Times.* https://www.nytimes.com/2019/09/17/style/generation-z-millennials-work-life-balance.html?fbclid=IwAR0O-t5P10PnmyZ40xmnXGOFwTDVejpM-WSPl3zNT7GX5OTc-XbogEKGF5oE.

"The Future Of Jobs Report 2018." 2019. *World Economic Forum.* http://www3.weforum.org/docs/WEF_Future_of_Jobs_2018.pdf.

Vasudeva, Payal, and Diana Barea. 2019. "Gen Z Rising." *Accenture.* https://www.accenture.com/_acnmedia/pdf-32/accenture-strategy-workforce-gen-z-rising-pov-uk.pdf.

Yudkowsky, Eliezer. 2001. Creating Friendly AI 1.0: The Analysis and Design of Benevolent Goal Architectures. The Singularity Institute, San Francisco, CA, June 15.

ACKNOWLEDGEMENTS

——

When I first sat down and began scribbling away ideas, I never expected to be publishing *The Z Factor* a few short months later. It took an incredible amount of effort to reach the end of this journey, not just from me, but from the many amazing people who have supported me along the way. Fulfilling this dream would not have been possible without you.

Thank you first and foremost to my mom, dad, and brother for guiding me through every step of the way, always. Whenever I got discouraged or felt like my writing wasn't going anywhere, you encouraged me to keep doing what I love.

Thank you to everyone at New Degree Press for helping me make this book a reality. To the publishing heads, Eric Koester and Brian Bies; my editors, Davida Smith-Keita, Leila

Summers, and Bailee Noella; and my book designers, Darja Filipovic and Gjorgji Pejkovski.

And thank you to everyone who gave me their time for a personal interview, pre-ordered the eBook, paperback, and multiple copies to make publishing possible, helped spread the word about *The Z Factor* to gather amazing momentum, and helped me publish a book I am proud of. I am sincerely grateful for all of your help.

Ogadimma Alilonu	Yoel Fiflezghi	Amani Phipps
Ben Baker	Megan Knauer	Alisha Pollastri
The Berry Family	Danae Koslovsky	Amal Pulikkiyil
Kavita Berry	Erica Langan	Kamal Rao
Jill Blythe	Franklin S Lee	Arden Reece
Lyndon Forbes Bowen	Novidha Lenin	Tyler Reiser
Siddharth Bowgal	Yashmitha Lenin	Ishwar Saini
Jack Boyd	Heather Li	The Shahi Family
Natasha Brown	Sonali Luthar	Sandeep Shahi
Arthur Canizares	Neha Majety	Sumit Sharma
Rosie Canizares	Michael Marino	Anand Sukka
Jake Cariello	Atul Maske	Kevin Sun
Lucas Carter	The Mathur Family	Alex VanderEls
Sudesh Chopra	Andrew May	Jatinder Vij
Eric Dai	Catherine McMillan	Melissa Wadley
Genesis Dawson	The Mehta Family	Dennis Wang

Magdalyn Foley

Swati Godbole

The Gulati Family

Amit Jain

Himanshu Jain

The Kakkar Family

Anand Nachiappan

Mary An Nan

Kush Patel

Priyam Patel

Carlos Peñaherrera

Braeden Ward

Darren White

Corrie Wiedmann

Luiza Wolf

Anna Xu

Made in the USA
Middletown, DE
08 June 2023

32250548R00106